The religion that captivated minds with its logic

By: Hatem Yahia

Contact: hat_em@hotmail.com

If you find this book to be interesting, please recommend it to your friends.

Hatem Yahia
Copyright 2016
Third edition

1

Table of Contents

Introduction

This book is based upon selected (translated) verses from the holy book, the Quran; verses that contain logical information or reasoning with the human mind. These verses indicate that Islam is a religion that respects, moreover rewards, thinking and contemplation. The Quran is a revelation from God, transported by the angel Gabriel, delivered to the Messenger Muhammad (may Allah bless him and grant him peace).

The verses present irrefutable logic that leave a person astonished as he gradually comprehends the weight of what he is presented with, leaving him thinking deeply. If a person truly grasps the logic, and is objective in his deductions without being hindered by pride, he will end up with just one sensible conclusion: belief in one God.

But to those who doubt that the verses are from God, it is up to them to decide whether these verses are within a human's capability and knowledge to compose or if they surpass human limits. I believe that within everyone is a God-given innate instinct that can recognize what is unique and sent from Him.

This book will be divided into sections, each section responding to a false claim or addressing a belief issue via simple logic provided in the Quran. This will begin by responding to the basic claim that there is no God, and progressing systematically through the sections to reach the final logical conclusion; the truth.

It is important to note that in the Quranic verses, terms used by God when describing Himself are often plural in the Arabic language, indicating greatness and extolment. For example, "We" and "Us" is used frequently instead of "I" or "Me". It is not a literal indication that God is a multiple entity.

NB. The endnotes indicate the source of the translation of the Quran verses, since the original Scripture of the Quran is in Arabic. As in regards to Prophet Muhammad's sayings (may Allah bless him and grant him peace), the endnotes indicate the narrator of the Hadeeth.

Chapter 1: Faulty reasoning in faith

The majority of people that fall into faulty beliefs are bound to one of two categories. These are either: disbelieving in God (atheism), or believing in God but accompanied by an association of partners with Him (polytheism). In the second category, the commonest finding is associating a son with God. These beliefs will be discussed in a purely rational and systematic manner within this chapter, so that the reader can think and decide for himself whether these beliefs are sensible or not.

1.1 Denying the existence of God

Individuals who don't believe in God do so based on an erred argument, resulting from uninformed aspects or misunderstood issues. Others may adhere to disbelief based on desire, while ignoring signs and what their deepest instincts whisper to them. If only they would pause from their lives every once in a while, slowing its pace down, and ponder in serenity...

Observe what's around, listen. Perceive

To every disbeliever, a basic issue must have presented itself: have you looked closely at what's around you and pondered, then got convinced that this is all a coincidence? The blue skies, the scurrying clouds, the flying birds, the tiny lively insects, the beautiful and astonishing variable sea creatures that live even in the deepest parts of the sea, the delicate patterns on butterflies and flowers and ladybugs, pointless?

The enormous planets orbiting around the sun in a balanced state, while each planet rotates around itself, with soothing beautiful moons rotating around them, and the thousands of shining stars, haphazardly? Consider the speed of an orbiting planet that is held by the centrifugal effect around the Sun, if its speed increases it will catapult out of the system, and if it slows down it will be drawn towards the Sun.

Moreover, a planet's course isn't perfectly circular, it is oval, causing its distance from the Sun to vary throughout the year. Add to all this that there are multiple planets orbiting around the Sun. For millions of years this balanced yet actively interacting system hasn't collapsed, all by chance? Can the probability of all these specific things happening by coincidence or natural evolution be calculated even?

How can this intricate and organized universe come into existence, and moreover order, without someone who intended it? If an individual saw a helicopter and asked who manufactured it, then someone answered "it just happened to be" or "it evolved to be so", would it be a convincing answer? Such detailed functionality and synchronicity cannot spur without being directed.

Furthermore, how can intelligent life-forms like insects, animals and humans come into existence from a non-intelligent source or process? God says about the creations around us '*Then do they not look at the camels - how they are created? [17] And at the sky - how it is raised? [18] And at the mountains - how they are erected? [19] And at the earth - how it is spread out?*' [88: 17–20][1].

And how can this universe persist so long without someone to preserve it from aberration? God preserves all these intricate and balanced creations lest they should deviate and then perish, which He informed us of '*Indeed, Allah holds the heavens and the earth, lest they cease. And if they should cease, no one could hold them [in place] after Him. Indeed, He is Forbearing and Forgiving*' [35: 41][1].

Even on a smaller scale, the Earth, humans have thrived upon it for thousands of years in spite of a condition where if one of the many large space bodies (such as an asteroid) hits Earth, we would perish no matter where it strikes. And about this point God states:

Have you not seen that Allah has subjected to you whatever is in the earth and the ships to run upon the sea (Literally: in the sea) at His Command, and He holds back the heaven so that it should not fall down upon the earth except by His permission? Surely Allah is indeed to mankind Ever-Compassionate, Ever-Merciful. [22: 65][3].

If a person says that this is all coincidental (or that nature caused it, which is the same as saying it is coincidental because nature isn't a lively entity in itself, it's a general term), it is a denial that there is greater meaning to living. This is because it would mean that there is no greater point to our (and all that's around us) existence, since all living things die, and that's it for them. However, our lives are not pointless, nor are the Heavens and Earth and all that's around us created pointlessly.

God stated to us a very reasonable point, that He didn't create all this just for enjoyment, there is some greater meaning to all of this '*We created not the heavens and the earth and all that is between them for a (mere) play. [16] Had We intended to take a pastime (i.e. a wife or a son, etc.), We could surely have taken it from Us, if We were going to do (that)*' [21: 16–17][2]. Indeed, God is exalted from doing trivial things such as creating the Heavens and the Earth aimlessly, or taking a wife or son. The purpose of creating all this is for Him to supervise each person's behaviour, and then to reward them according to their actions:

And We did not create the heaven and the earth and that between them aimlessly. That is the assumption of those who disbelieve, so woe to those who disbelieve from the Fire. [27] Or should we treat those who believe and do righteous deeds like corrupters in the land? Or should We treat those who fear Allah like the wicked? [38: 27–28][1].

This statement also annuls the assumption, which some people have, that there is a God who created this world but then becomes just a passive observer, i.e. leaving creatures do as they wish and events occurring without interference, since this would mean that God did something aimless. This is an inappropriate characteristic to exist in a Lord, and is -in practicality- similar to assuming that there is no God since it is an assumption that God will do nothing.

Furthermore, leaving oppressors to do injustice upon others (and ultimately get away with it) without interference from the All-Powerful God, who is capable to enforce justice, would mean that God concurs this injustice, another feature that is inappropriate to be found in God. If a policeman sees a crime occurring in front of him and chooses not to interfere then isn't he part of that crime? The explanation that injustice is left to occur in this world is that God ruled that He will effectuate ultimate justice in the Hereafter, after He records irrefutable proof of what everyone actually did. As for this life, God intervenes sometimes to return some people's rights, but usually after a delay.

To those who deny that there is a God, He says this to them '*And have they not looked into the Dominion of the heavens and the earth and what things Allah has created, and that may be that their term has already drawn near? So, in whichever discourse after (this) are they to believe?*' [7: 185][3]. So look again, '*Do they not see the birds held (flying) in the midst of the sky? None holds them but Allah [none gave them the ability to fly but Allah]. Verily, in this are clear proofs and signs for people who believe (in the Oneness of Allah)*' [16: 79][2].

And look again and again '*Who has created the seven heavens one above another, you can see no fault in the creations of the Most Beneficent. Then look again: "Can you see any rifts?" [3] Then look again and yet again, your sight will return to you in a state of humiliation and worn out*' [67: 3–4][2]. Check the skies for any fissures, your eyesight will get fatigued before you find any.

The reality of the situation is that all living, and even inanimate, things that God created submit to Him in obedience and exalt Him. It is just that we don't understand their exaltations, for different species have different methods assigned to it:

Do you not see that Allah is exalted by whomever is within the heavens and the earth and [by] the birds with wings spread [in flight]? Each [of them] has known his [means of] prayer and exalting [Him], and Allah is Knowing of what they do. [41] And to Allah belongs the dominion of the heavens and the earth, and to Allah is the destination. [24: 41–42][1].

And this is a matter of fact, for God reveals to us an example of the method of prostration '*Have they not considered what things Allah has created? Their shadows incline to the right and to the left, prostrating to Allah, while they are humble*' [16: 48][1]. So this is a method of prostration regarding inanimate creations that God assigned to them.

It must be pointed out that God loves to be praised particularly during two phases in the day: sunrise and sunset. And He informed Prophet Muhammad (may Allah bless him and grant him peace) about this, so Muslims recite their praises especially during these two times of the day (praising should not be confused with praying). Is it coincidental then that we hear the greatest chirping for birds at these times? Is it coincidental that tree leaves and flowers open at sunrise and close at sunset?

A disbeliever may attribute all these phenomena to the Sun's state, but then who created the Sun, and who designed these creatures to respond to the Sun!? God informs us '*And to Allah prostrate themselves whoever are in the heavens and the earth, willingly and unwillingly, and their shadows (prostrate) in the early mornings and (the hours) before sunset. [A prostration is to be performed here]*' [13: 15][2].

Do we not notice the behavioural differences in animals and plants at these times? It is because many people look but do not see, hear but do not listen, recognize but do not accept; for some do not ponder, whilst others choose denial over belief and ignorance over knowledge. Do we have to understand how other creatures praise God in order to acknowledge that it happens? How so when even people of different cultures do not understand each other due to lingual differences, although they are the very same species?

It is not our place, nor within our capability, to comprehend all the different ways that all the various creatures have been assigned to praise God. What concerns us is our assignment in worshipping Him, and it is not for us to speculate sceptically over other creations, because our non-comprehension of the praises performed by the creatures does not mean it doesn't happen.

God informs us '*The seven heavens and the earth and whatever is in them exalt Him. And there is not a thing except that it exalts [Allah] by His praise, but you do not understand their [way of] exalting. Indeed, He is ever Forbearing and Forgiving*' [17: 44][1]. So all that is around us, and the spike in activity of creatures during sunrise and sunset, is not nature's doing, nor is it coincidental; God's hand is apparent in His creation.

But alas, disbelievers claim that there is no proof of God's existence, whilst they pass by hundreds of signs daily, such as the sun, clouds, birds, moon and stars. God states one such basic sign saying '*Do you not see that Allah has sent down rain from the sky and the earth becomes green? Indeed, Allah is Subtle and Acquainted.*' [22: 63][1]. Truly it is fascinating and beautiful how the soil turns lively with green vegetation after rainy seasons.

Another example that is presented to us is '*And within the land are neighboring plots and gardens of grapevines and crops and palm trees, [growing] several from a root or otherwise, watered with one water; but We make some of them exceed others in [quality of] fruit. Indeed in that are signs for a people who reason.*' [13: 4][1].

All the plants have one food source and one fluid source (soil and water), yet each seed expresses a different set of fruit, leaf and stem pattern. All such information is stored within each seed. Thus two neighbouring plants, when fed the same water, may produce entirely different fruits just because the programming within each seed is different. How can this be unintentional?

And this variation is not limited to plants, which God states. *'Do you not see that Allah sends down rain from the sky, and We produce thereby fruits of varying colors? And in the mountains are tracts, white and red of varying shades and [some] extremely black. [27] And among people and moving creatures and grazing livestock are various colors similarly. Only those fear Allah, from among His servants, who have knowledge. Indeed, Allah is Exalted in Might and Forgiving.'* [35: 27–28][1].

But some people attribute this phenomenon to evolution instead of God. However, attributing this variation to evolution does not logically answer a very critical question: How did the very first living cell, from which everything theoretically evolved, come into existence? From what substance did it emerge?

Furthermore, if the goal of evolution is to ensure survival of life through advancement and variation of species throughout generations, it does not make sense for it to end up with different species feeding upon others. This situation would mean that evolution is eating itself from within.

The reality of the situation is that disbelievers are between being oblivious to God's signs or in denial that they are from God, taking them for granted. So God sums up their state *'And how many a sign within the heavens and earth do they pass over while they, therefrom, are turning away.'* [12: 105][1].

On a related topic about the creation of the universe, a very tricky issue that some doubters may present onto people is: If God created everything, who then created God? The answer, simply and briefly put, is none (we can't even say He created Himself, it is inappropriate as will be explained).

Logically put, we cannot assess God on the parameters of us humans, for He is far greater than to be compatibly measured by our standards and definitions. This is because we are bound by parameters which He isn't bound by (e.g. time, space, eating, sleeping, physical strength and so on).

How can we measure His features when the very foundations of His essence are dissimilar from us, for when He wills to create something or make something happen, all that occurs is that He says to it: Be; and so it becomes. Nothing is similar to Him in any aspect.

Furthermore, our minds aren't that advanced to fully comprehend His features. It is like expecting a computer with artificial intelligence to comprehend how humans survive without recharging with electricity, which is impossible since the computer never experienced eating. Moreover, if it comes in contact with water it will deteriorate.

The computer can just memorize this information after being informed about it. Similarly, what we know about God is only what He informed us about in His holy book and through His prophets; and we have no capability to speculate about Him.

In the end of this subsection, it must be pointed out that in Islam, in contrast to most of the other religions, free thinking about the universe is not only allowed, but moreover encouraged. This is because the truth doesn't fear being subjected to inquisitions and tests; unlike injustice and falsehood, which evade being exposed to light. Hence, God encourages people to think, research and ask questions about what exists around them, since their findings will help them ascertain that there must be a God to all this. Additionally, doing so will help them comprehend, to some extent, His greatness.

These findings will also concur with what is in the Quran, thus proving more that God exists and that this book is from Him, which increases the faith of the thinkers. So God urges us to think:

Indeed, in the creation of the heavens and the earth and the alternation of the night and the day are signs for those of understanding. [190] Who remember Allah while standing or sitting or [lying] on their sides and give thought to the creation of the heavens and the earth, [saying], "Our Lord, You did not create this aimlessly; exalted are You [above such a thing]; then protect us from the punishment of the Fire. [3: 190–191][1].

Then, look into yourselves

God displayed the signs of His existence and Oneness not only in what's around us, but even within our very selves, all so we can realize His existence. He says '*And on the earth are signs for the certain [in faith] [20] And in yourselves. Then will you not see?*' [50: 20–21][1].

Some people ponder about themselves from the spiritual perspective, wondering what the ulterior purpose of their life is. Others ponder from the physical perspective, such as how do they have control over their hands and legs, and how their bodies are formed with consideration down to the smallest details. The fine functional details include the white blood cells and chemicals released to induce emotional and physical changes. These people may discover that all of these rivers of deep thought have one feature in common.

The common feature is that all of them pour down into the same sea: that there must be a God; then some accept this fact whilst others reject it. As an example, God directs us to think about our nature, starting with the nature of what our very own bodies emit (the sperms in human semen), of which the difference between us and them is the appointed time of death. Some die before us whilst others become the next generation and die after us:

Have you seen that which you emit? [58] Is it you who creates it, or are We the Creator? [59] We have decreed death among you, and We are not to be outdone [60] In that We will change your likenesses and produce you in that [form] which you do not know. [61] And you have already known the first creation, so will you not remember? [62] And have you seen that [seed] which you sow? [63] Is it you who makes it grow, or are We the grower? [64] If We willed, We could make it [dry] debris, and you would remain in wonder, [65] [Saying], "Indeed, we are [now] in debt; [66] Rather, we have been deprived." [67] And have you seen the water that you drink? [68] Is it you who brought it down from the clouds, or is it We who bring it down? [69] If We willed, We could make it bitter, so why are you not grateful? [70] And have you seen the fire that you ignite? [71] Is it you who produced its tree, or are We the producer? [72] We have made it a reminder and provision for the travelers, [73] So exalt the name

of your Lord, the Most Great. [56: 58–74][1].

Moving on to another issue, a very baffling phenomena that many disbelievers overlook is how their lives are spent doing what God programmed their bodies to do, and yet they deny God's existence. To clarify, the human is designed to eat, drink, sleep at night, acquire a home for shelter, fear death and search for his other half (soul mate, i.e. wife or husband).

For example, when a suicidal individual is at the brink of killing himself (e.g. at the edge of a cliff or holding a gun to his head), tremendous fear from dying overwhelms him although he is convinced that he needs to take this step. So why is this so? Who programmed this self-preservation in us, that fear from death kicks in even if an individual is convinced that he needs to kill himself? God informed us that this is what we are bound by because He designed us like that.

This was evident in many verses like '*Do they not see that We made the night that they may rest therein and the day giving sight? Indeed in that are signs for a people who believe.*' [27: 86][1]; '*And of His signs is that He created you from dust; then, suddenly you were human beings dispersing [throughout the earth]. [20] And of His signs is that He created for you from yourselves mates that you may find tranquillity in them; and He placed between you affection and mercy. Indeed in that are signs for a people who give thought.*' [30: 20–21][1]. Upon such, shouldn't a person first be able to break away from the path which God dictated his body to follow, in order to credibly say that there is no God who programmed him?

Ending this subsection with an interesting story, a pious man was once asked: with what did you ascertain (the existence of) your God?

He replied: from the revoking of determinations and annulment of plans! What he meant is that a person determines and plans to get something done, something that no other human desires to stop, and yet all his plans fail mysteriously and his persistence is fruitless, leaving the person puzzled.

In other words, it happens that a person wills to do something and plans it perfectly, but God wills otherwise. So, unexpected incidents (to the person) keep arising in every step that disarray his arrangements and unwind his accomplishments at almost every level; making the person's will void and his efforts futile, while God implements His will.

Conclusively, if there was no God, every plan that a man thoroughly makes that does not conflict with another man's plan would be accomplished without exception. However, it is evident that there is a higher will than a human's will that keep altering plans in a manner that is beyond coincidence.

A futuristic fact that is proven logically

God says '*How can you disbelieve in Allah when you were lifeless and He brought you to life; then He will cause you to die, then He will bring you [back] to life, and then to Him you will be returned*' [2: 28][1]. And this is a very enlightening fact that makes us contemplate: we were a nonentity before we were born, created from nothing and given life. We then die on Earth and will all be resurrected on a due day, ultimately returning to Him to be judged on what we did on Earth.

Even to those who argue saying "we know we were nothing before and then came to life, and we know we will die, but we do not believe that in the future we will be resurrected because there is no evidence for that", there is proof. The fact that we will be resurrected is proven in the very same verse by the fact that it happened before. We were nothing and then we were given life, so what is there to prevent it from happening again?

So the single verse contains a futuristic fact and its proof, which is above a human's capacity in composition, therefore pointing to the presence of a God who compiled such a powerful self-proving and decisive verse. And the question in the verse "how can you disbelieve in Allah" stresses on how disbelieving is a very irrational thing to do in spite of the given facts.

The extinction of previous civilizations; a sign?

It is puzzling, how can the perishing of previous civilizations be proof of God's presence? A person needs to look at this phenomenon from a specific angle, with scientific reasoning. The sign is not that there are previous civilizations that have perished mysteriously, nor is it that some disbelieving civilizations perished whilst others haven't, but rather that ALL the historic civilizations that perished were disbelievers!

Never once has it happened that a civilization that truly believed in God (by being expressed in their actions, serving as proof of truthful belief) had been subjected to God's wrath and perished, for why would God perish a civilization that believes in Him? *'What can Allah gain by your punishment, if ye are grateful and ye believe? Nay, it is Allah that recogniseth (all good), and knoweth all things'* [4: 147][2]. All previous believing societies that perished have disintegrated first internally (i.e. drifted from God's path and went astray), and only then did they perish.

So from a scientific point of view, the fact that all the civilizations that perished were disbelievers and none were believers denotes what is termed a 'significant pattern' (i.e. an evident correlation). And it is this pattern that God presents to the disbelievers as a logical argument in that they should believe in Him *'Not one of the towns (populations), of those which We destroyed, believed before them (though We sent them signs), will they then believe?'* [21: 6][2]. And God calls upon the people's minds and hearts so that they believe, saying:

And how many a city did We destroy while it was committing wrong - so it is [now] fallen into ruin - and [how many] an abandoned well and [how many] a lofty palace. [45] So have they not traveled through the earth and have hearts by which to reason and ears by which to hear? For indeed, it is not eyes that are blinded, but blinded are the hearts which are within the breasts [22: 45–46][1].

"Blinded are the hearts" refers to the hatred and arrogance in the hearts that prevent them from seeing the truth, or more precisely, from accepting the truth. And in a chain of mesmerizing verses, God disdains those who disbelieve, mock and laugh scornfully at what the Prophet Muhammad (may Allah bless him and grant him peace) is saying in spite of all the signs:

Did you (O Muhammad SAW) observe him who turned away (from Islam). [33] And gave a little, then stopped (giving)? [34] Is with him the knowledge of the unseen so that he sees? [35] Or is he not informed with what is in the Pages (Scripture) of Musa (Moses), [36] And of Ibrahim (Abraham) who fulfilled (or conveyed) all that (what Allah ordered him to do or convey), [37] That no burdened person (with sins) shall bear the burden (sins) of another. [38] And that man can have nothing but what he does (good or bad). [39] And that his deeds will be seen, [40] Then he will be recompensed with a full and the best recompense. [41] And that to your Lord (Allah) is the End (Return of everything). [42] And that it is He (Allah) Who makes (whom He wills) laugh, and makes (whom He wills) weep; [43] And that it is He (Allah) Who causes death and gives life; [44] And that He (Allah) creates the pairs, male and female, [45] From Nutfah (drops of semen male and female discharges) when it is emitted; [46] And that upon Him (Allah) is another bringing forth (Resurrection); [47] And that it is He (Allah) Who gives much or a little (or gives wealth and contentment), [48] And that He (Allah) is the Lord of Sirius (the star which the pagan Arabs used to worship); [49] And that it is He (Allah) Who destroyed the former 'Ad (people), [50] And Thamud (people). He spared none of them. [51] And the people of Nuh (Noah) aforetime, verily, they were more unjust and more rebellious and transgressing [in disobeying Allah and His Messenger Nuh (Noah)]. [52] And He destroyed the overthrown cities [of Sodom to which Prophet

Lout (Lot) was sent]. [53] So there covered them that which did cover (i.e. torment with stones). [54] Then which of the Graces of your Lord (O man!) will you doubt. [55] This (Muhammad SAW) is a warner (Messenger) of the (series of) warners (Messengers) of old. [56] The Day of Resurrection draws near, [57] None besides Allah can avert it, (or advance it, or delay it). [58] Do you then wonder at this recital (the Quran)? [59] And you laugh at it and weep not, [60] Wasting your (precious) lifetime in pastime and amusements (singing, etc.). [61] So fall you down in prostration to Allah, and worship Him (Alone). [53: 33–62][2].

And from a logical perspective, if there were cities of believers that God had perished, wouldn't that cause virtuousness to be eliminated from the face of the Earth? In other words, perishing believers would leave disbelievers to flourish, which would eventually lead to the wiping of God's word from the face of the Earth. So does it make sense that God would eliminate His own word after it has been established on Earth? Never once has God annihilated a believing city.

On a side note regarding this topic, some people disbelieve in God or bear ill-feelings to Him on account that He allows suffering to befall (even to good/innocent people). Some even go as far as accusing God for causing this evil, forgetting the fact that God left us to do what we want in this life as a documented test, which entitles that some people perform evil, harming others in their path.

On the other hand, clarifying why God subjects people to hardships, or allows the evil caused from immoral individuals to reach other people, needs extensive explanation. Aside from the verses just mentioned that it is illogical that God would perish truly virtuous people, the reasons for hardships must be understood. Initially, it must be noted that the reasons for hardships don't all fall under the same category; the purpose may be for testing, refinement or punishment.

Firstly, when bad things befall good people, it is a test for them, to see if they will stick to the path of God or if they will resent and be discontent, using this hardship as an excuse to commit violations and become immoral. So hardships separate those who are virtuous under any circumstance (these have the highest rank from God in the Hereafter) from the other groups.

The other groups include those who have no patience (who revert to being good after the hardship passes), and below them all is the group containing individuals that claim virtuousness by mouth but are actually evil all the time. We should keep remembering that our life on Earth is but a test, so when a tough question comes in a test to segregate the unique from the good, are we to be shocked and resentful?

Suffice to say that for every suffering a pious person endures, he will be abundantly compensated for it by God in the Hereafter, to such an extent that the pious person will be left feeling and knowing that he is a winner. This occurs due to the fact that God keeps rewarding that person even after ascertaining that the compensation he received is valued to be much more than for the suffering he endured.

It reaches a degree where the pious person wishes he had more hardships in his life! This way, justice has been established. Thus the bigger the hardship is, the greater the compensation becomes. As a definite example, those who were poor in life enter Heaven before the rich up to 500 years earlier, which is multiply longer than a life span spent being poor.

This aspect of hardship is especially apparent in cases such as children who were subject to injustices from people or struck by natural disasters. Those who die from such hardships are compensated by entering Heaven directly without going through the judgement process, since they didn't reach the age of accountability for their actions to God. Moreover, they hold their parents' hands and escort them into Heaven (those of which believe in God), in compensation for what the parents endured due to the parting of their children.

Secondly, there is the refinement aspect of hardships, since the person evolves and becomes stronger and more experienced about life, by becoming more patient and more insightful. For example, he learns who his true friends are, since they are the ones who stand by him in hardships, and learns modesty and compassion with those in hardships since he comprehends their suffering more. This aspect is similar to how the army subjects its soldiers to repeated exercises of endurance so that they develop higher capabilities.

Lastly, who of us really never disobeys God? If any of us is convinced of this, then he is either lying to himself or is unaware that he is sinning. Even to a person who disbelieves in God and the concept of sins, it must've happened that he committed an action which he himself testifies that wronged a specific person, ultimately feeling shame from it. God created man flawed and with the ability to defy Him, thus man is bound to disobey God whether impulsively or resolutely. The actuality of what is required from man is to resist sinning, and when he commits a sin, he is expected to truthfully repent. Thus, these bad incidents purify us from our wrong deeds (the punishment aspect of hardships).

That last aspect of hardship is straightforwardly mentioned to us. God says *'Corruption has appeared throughout the land and sea by [reason of] what the hands of people have earned so He may let them taste part of [the consequence of] what they have done that perhaps they will return [to righteousness]'* [30: 41][1].

And let us be honest with ourselves, hardships make people turn to God when they wouldn't have otherwise pleaded and resorted to Him. God loves to forgive and grant His slaves their requests, but He wills to hear us request it from Him, and then He grants it so easily. These hardships sometimes serve as a reminder to us that we have drifted away from God, and maybe even make us come to terms with ourselves that we have deserted God's path long enough.

On a related topic, some disbelievers say that if God does exist, He will judge people on how good they were irrespective of their belief in Him, and will let the good people enter Heaven. The reality of the situation is that this is not rational, because He set a prerequisite that for someone to enter Heaven: he should believe in God and obey Him. It is His Heaven, and therefore His rules apply.

It is irrational for a person to expect to get an invitation from a house owner, for a gathering, not only after disrespecting the owner's house rules, but moreover after declaring that he doesn't believe that this house belongs to its owner. And how could someone honourably accept and have the face to enter God's Heaven after he had insistently rejected acknowledging God!?

That person did not give God His right of worship, yet gave people their rights (according to his own subjective rules and self-evaluation/judgement), and expects to enter Heaven upon that. It is like giving a poor man a fortune that was stolen from a rich man in an attempt by the thief to repent. How does this return the rights of the rich man, and how has justice been enacted on the thief?

Daring the befall of vengeance as a proof of God's existence

There is a faction of disbelievers who have reached a level of hard-headedness and audacity that they dared Prophet Muhammad (as with the Prophets before him, may Allah grant them peace) to send down God's punishment upon them if what he is saying is true. Those people have reached a level of arrogance and irrationality that they ask for God's punishment as proof instead of a clear yet harmless sign for them to believe. So I ask the reader, what level of irrationality is that?

And God points out the main flaw in their request *'Say, "Have you considered: if His punishment should come to you by night or by day - for which [aspect] of it would the criminals be impatient?" [50] Then is it that when it has [actually] occurred you will believe in it? Now? And you were [once] for it impatient'* [10: 50–51][1]. And so, this is the main contradiction in their request, they will believe only when the punishment befalls, and yet when it befalls, God does not accept any repentance at that time, nor does He lift the punishment. That is what He decreed and warned of:

Do they then wait for anything other than that the angels should come to them, or that your Lord should come, or that some of the Signs of your Lord should come (i.e. portents of the Hour e.g., arising of the sun from the west)! The day that some of the Signs of your Lord do come, no good will it do to a person to believe then, if he believed not before, nor earned good (by performing deeds of righteousness) through his Faith. Say: "Wait you! we (too) are waiting." [6: 158][2].

Another contradiction in their request is that they are certain that punishment will not befall them on Earth for their defiance. This when if they had assessed the overall situation thoroughly, they would have reached the conclusion that this life is mainly a test phase and not a punishment phase. How? God stated a peculiar fact *'And if Allah were to punish men for that which they earned, He would not leave a moving (living) creature on the surface of the earth, but He gives them respite to an appointed term, and when their term comes, then verily, Allah is Ever AllSeer of His slaves.'* [35: 45][2].

If God were to punish every person on Earth due to his sins, then there would not be a single person left on Earth currently. This is because every single person falls into sins, even those who believe in God may fall into a grave sin at one point in their lives. But the continuation of the test leads to two conclusions, firstly that this life is not the main place for punishment upon deeds. This means that even if a disbeliever turns out to be wrong and there is a God, the befalling of severe punishment is not a must, since this is the test phase where individuals are allowed the full chance. It is the afterlife that is the punishment and reward phase.

Secondly, the verse indicates that sinning isn't the top issue that God is testing us upon, since He hasn't wiped out mankind and the Earth yet. The reality is that the main test issue is to see who will disbelieve in Him.

And yet another contradiction in the request is that when their fate hits them (judgement), and reality imposes itself upon them (punishment), they will undoubtedly ask for more time to fix their state after they awaited punishment. This after being given a full term *'They will not believe in it until they see the painful punishment. [201] And it will come to them suddenly while they perceive [it] not. [202] And they will say, "May we be reprieved?"* [26: 201–203][1].

A logical question then remains: suppose the punishment is delayed and they enjoy life to the maximal as they wished, and moreover God gives them all the prosperity they wanted, what good will that be in front of eternal punishment if it exists? *'So, do they seek to hasten Our torment? [204] Then, have you seen, in case We give them enjoyment for (many) years, [205] Thereafter (there) comes to them what they have been promised, [206] In no way will avail them whatever they had been given to enjoy.'* [26: 204–207][2].

But even before the grave punishment befalls, do we not notice how minuscule we are in this Universe, and how common grand events which can be life threatening if altered, such as lightning and blizzards, are so easily done by God? It comes:

Do you not see that Allah drives clouds? Then He brings them together, then He makes them into a mass, and you see the rain emerge from within it. And He sends down from the sky, mountains [of clouds] within which is hail, and He strikes with it whom He wills and averts it from whom He wills. The flash of its lightening almost takes away the eyesight. [43] Allah alternates the night and the day. Indeed in that is a lesson for those who have vision. [24: 43–44][1].

However, usually for those who reach this level of defiance, no matter how many or how clear the signs are, they are so lost within their pride and so blinded by their desires that that they will never believe. That is so until they evaluate the punishment by themselves or witness the first incident demarcating the initiation of judgement day.

The primary incident is the rise of the sun from where it sets (west), whence everyone will believe, but it will be too late for a change in the stance on belief to matter.

And God comforts Muhammad (may Allah bless him and grant him peace) over this fact, that some individuals will never believe him because they are too immoral, since he used to grieve over the souls that he couldn't save. God foretold him about those people *'Indeed, those upon whom the word of your Lord has come into effect will not believe, [96] Even if every sign should come to them, until they see the painful punishment'* [10: 96–97][1].

This is because, as God tells Muhammad (may Allah bless him and grant him peace), they have taken their desires as Gods (i.e. their guide and priority), so there is nothing he can do for them. The prophet's responsibility is just to deliver the message, and rather it is them that should resolve to change themselves. God enlightened us saying *'Hast thou seen him who chooseth for his god his own lust? Wouldst thou then be guardian over him?'* [25: 43][4].

This is the state regarding individuals who reach a level of arrogance and commit so many atrocities to the extent that God 'stamps' on their hearts to stay blind to the truth. They are so lost that they perceive their evil actions as beneficial to the society, even reaching the delusion that it pleases God if He does exist! God described their state asking:

Then is one to whom the evil of his deed has been made attractive so he considers it good [like one rightly guided]? For indeed, Allah sends astray whom He wills and guides whom He wills. So do not let yourself perish over them in regret. Indeed, Allah is Knowing of what they do. [35: 8][1]. Truly, theirs is a sorrowful state.

To such stubborn people, a warning like this is befitting *'Seest thou not that Allah created the heavens and the earth in Truth? If He so will, He can remove you and put (in your place) a new creation? [19] Nor is that for Allah any great matter'* [14: 19–20][2]. And such an event has befallen previously. Have we not seen entire advanced civilizations (such as the Pharaohs and Aztecs) wiped out in spite of their advancements, with only monuments and fossils remaining where they dwelled to prove their historical existence?

And later on, ironically, does it not happen that another civilization comes to populate their site and claim they are stronger and more advanced? Yet the logical argument still remains *'Then do they await except that the Hour should come upon them unexpectedly? But already there have come [some of] its indications. Then what good to them, when it has come, will be their remembrance?'* [47: 18][1].

There is neither a resurrection nor a judgment day?

This assumption goes hand in hand with disbelieving in God, since disbelieving in the Hereafter fundamentally requires denying God's ability to resurrect and recompense. The issue is in that denying any of God's abilities is describing Him as incomplete, which is (practically) disbelief in God as He really is. But this is what God says to those who disbelieve in resurrection for judgement:

And they say, "When we are bones and crumbled particles, will we [truly] be resurrected as a new creation?" [49] Say, "Be you stones or iron, [50] Or [any] creation of that which is great within your breasts." And they will say, "Who will restore us?" Say, "He who brought you forth the first time." Then they will nod their heads toward you and say, "When is that?" Say, "Perhaps it will be soon – [51] On the Day He will call you and you will respond with praise of Him and think that you had not remained [in the world] except for a little." [17: 49–52][1].

This is the truth, that just like He brought them into existence in the first place, He can revive them. This is very logical because, practically speaking, reconstructing something is much easier than creating it out of nothing; but all the matters are easy and all are the same to God. He revives them just by His ordering: Be; and hence their bodies reassemble, and that is how powerful God is.

On a side note, people should realize that life on Earth is short. Even if someone lives to be a 100 years, when compared to the Hereafter (in which some days are equivalent to our 50,000 years) he will feel as if he lived for a few days or less. It is somewhat similar to how elderly people perceive their childhood, that it lasted very shortly.

And why is it so hard to believe that there is a resurrection when God questions us '*Were We then worn out by the first creation? Yet they are in doubt about a new creation*' [50: 15][4]. So even if God willed to create a new creation, He could, like He did the first time, but He wills to resurrect us in order to recompense us.

But some disbelievers keep ridiculing those who say there is a resurrection. God condemns their behaviour of arguing about His signs when just some years back, that person was nothing but a mere drop of sperm. So He confronts them, is the creation of what is around them harder or creating a muddy fluid?

Then inquire of them, [O Muhammad], "Are they a stronger [or more difficult] creation or those [others] We have created?" Indeed, We created men from sticky clay. [11] But you wonder, while they mock, [12] And when they are reminded, they remember not. [13] And when they see a sign, they ridicule [14] And say, "This is not but obvious magic. [15] When we have died and become dust and bones, are we indeed to be resurrected? [16] And our forefathers [as well]?" [37: 11–17][1].

Moreover, before he became an embryo, he didn't even exist and no one knew him nor mentioned him! '*Has there [not] come upon man a period of time when he was not a thing [even] mentioned?*' [49: 1][1]. God reminds the disbeliever about this, for he may deter from his stubbornness, presenting him with a logical question:

Does man not consider that We created him from a [mere] sperm-drop - then at once he is a clear adversary? [77] And he presents for Us an example and forgets his [own] creation. He says, "Who will give life to bones while they are disintegrated?" [78] Say, "He will give them life who produced them the first time; and He is, of all creation, Knowing." [79] [It is] He who made for you from the green tree, fire, and then from it you ignite. [80] Is not He who created the heavens and the earth Able to create the likes of them? Yes, [it is so]; and He is the Knowing Creator. [81] His command is only when He intends a thing that He says to it, "Be," and it is. [82] So exalted is He in whose hand is the realm of all things, and to Him you will be returned. [36: 77–83][1].

To confirm it to them more through signs they can see, God said:

See they not how Allah originates creation, then repeats it. Verily, that is easy for Allah. [19] Say: "Travel in the land and see how (Allah) originated creation, and then Allah will bring forth (resurrect) the creation of the Hereafter (i.e. resurrection after death). Verily, Allah is Able to do all things." [29: 19–20][2].

And this is the reality, that God repeats creation right in front of our eyes every day, but we do not realize it. When apples bud out of trees and are then eaten (or disintegrate), and new apples then sprout, isn't this cycle a repetition of creation? Even the very elements in the apple which was eaten, it will recycle into nutrients for a tree to produce another apple from. In another chapter, God gives more details about how people will be resurrected to the scornful disbelievers who ask in contempt:

"When we have died and have become dust, [we will return to life]? That is a distant return." [3] We know what the earth diminishes of them, and with Us is a retaining record. [4] But they denied the truth when it came to them, so they are in a confused condition. [5] Have they not looked at the heaven above them - how We structured it and adorned it and [how] it has no rifts? [6] And the earth - We spread it out and cast therein firmly set mountains and made grow therein [something] of every beautiful kind, [7] Giving insight and a reminder for every servant who turns [to Allah]. [8] And We have sent down blessed rain from the sky and

made grow thereby gardens and grain from the harvest [9] And lofty palm trees having fruit arranged in layers – [10] As provision for the servants, and We have given life thereby to a dead land. Thus is the resurrection. [50: 3–11][1].

We see it but do not connect the dots (tying this phenomenon to causation from God and how we are created), and similarly to this process God will resurrect all who died. So how can anyone accept repetition but reject resurrection when the processes are very similar!? Furthermore, it is very strange that some people perceive it difficult to them (as humans) to be reassembled and resurrected in spite of the fact that God created what is more complex and massive than human creation! '*Indeed the creation of the heavens and the earth is greater than the creation of mankind; but most of mankind do not know*' [40: 57][2].

In more detailed verses, God displays to us the creation of aspects of the universe, and asks us whether we imagine are we a more sophisticated creation than the skies, as an example. God says:

Are you a more difficult creation or is the heaven? Allah constructed it. [27] He raised its ceiling and proportioned it. [28] And He darkened its night and extracted its brightness. [29] And after that He spread the earth. [30] He extracted from it its water and its pasture, [31] And the mountains He set firmly [32] As provision for you and your grazing livestock. [79: 27–33][1] (Heaven here refers to the sky). He created all this for us, though we are a simpler creation than that which He created for us! We, in turn, should contemplate why.

And yet there are insistent people who still disbelieve. So God warns them, especially those who talked condescendingly to the Prophet for warning them that the resurrection will occur:

And he whom Allah guides, he is led aright; but he whom He sends astray for such you will find no Auliya' (helpers and protectors, etc.) besides Him, and We shall gather them together on the Day of Resurrection on their faces; blind, dumb and deaf, their abode will be Hell; whenever it abates, We shall increase for them the fierceness of the Fire. [97] That is their recompense, because they denied Our Ayat (proofs, evidences, verses, lessons, signs, revelations, etc.) and said: "When we are bones and fragments, shall we really be raised up as a new creation?" [98] See they not that Allah, Who created the heavens and the earth, is Able to create the like of them. And He has decreed for them an appointed term, whereof there is not doubt. But the Zalimun (polytheists and wrong-doers, etc.) refuse (the truth the Message of Islamic Monotheism, and accept nothing) but disbelief. [17: 97–99][2].

Still warningly, God presents a reminder to the disbelievers of how and what they originated from, and that it is illogical for them to be left without reckoning. He states:

Does man think that he will be left neglected? [36] Had he not been a sperm from semen emitted? [37] Then he was a clinging clot, and [Allah] created [his form] and proportioned [him] [38] And made of him two mates, the male and the female. [39] Is not that [Creator] Able to give life to the dead? [75: 36–40][1].

These verses raise another point, that man knows he developed into his current build and strength from that fluid, so why does he find it irrational that he can be reassembled from the dust which he will turn into? And in another chapter, God again forewarns after presenting them with a logical question:

And the disbeliever says, "When I have died, am I going to be brought forth alive?" [66] Does man not remember that We created him before, while he was nothing? [67] So by your Lord, We will surely gather them and the devils; then We will bring them to be present around Hell upon their knees. [68] Then We will surely extract from every sect those of them who were worst against the Most Merciful in insolence. [69] Then, surely it is We who are most knowing of those most worthy of burning therein. [19: 66–70][1].

In these verses, God contrasts His most prominent attribute, which is mercy, with the severity of His punishment; that although He is very merciful, yet with those individuals He will be very tormenting. He will treat them so because they trampled over all the boundaries and abused His graciousness. This contrasting is something that truly incites fear from His wrath.

Such disrespectful individuals exist now and existed at the time of the Prophets (may Allah grant them peace). God gives an example of one of them who was so arrogant and stubborn that he disbelieved in the Quran and the Prophet Muhammad (may Allah bless him and grant him peace), and yet coupled that with an audacious assertion.

His audacious assertion was that even if he is to be resurrected, he would be given wealth and be honoured, on account that he was given blessings on Earth which he was convinced he deserved. Where did he get the boldness to assert that just as God favoured him on Earth, God will definitely favour him in the Hereafter? He disbelieved that there is just one God and that there will be a resurrection, and yet expects to be rewarded in the Hereafter if he were to be resurrected, which is extremely contradictory. God informs us:

Have you seen him who disbelieved in Our Ayat (this Quran and Muhammad SAW) and (yet) says: "I shall certainly be given wealth and children [if I will be alive (again)]," [77] Has he known the unseen or has he taken a covenant from the Most Beneficent (Allah)? [78] Nay! We shall record what he says, and We shall increase his torment (in the Hell); [79] And We shall inherit from him (at his death) all that he talks of (i.e. wealth and children which We have bestowed upon him in this world), and he shall come to Us alone. [80] And they have taken (for worship) aliha (gods) besides Allah, that they might give them honour, power and glory (and also protect them from Allah's Punishment etc.). [81] Nay, but they (the so-called gods) will deny their worship of them, and become opponents to them (on the Day of Resurrection). [19: 77–82][2].

Overall, the reality of the situation is that most people know very well about worldly matters. They know well how to earn a living and accumulate wealth through various professions, such as engineering, law and trade, but don't know about (let alone attending to) their Hereafter matters as well as their worldly matters.

To clarify, many people know how to dress elegantly, how to lose weight, and how to apply cosmetics; but how many know the principles of interaction with people that fulfil treating them justly and with respect? How many know that it is wrong to whisper to someone in the presence of a third individual?

How many know what percent of their wealth are they supposed to donate to the poor and with what frequency? Some readers may have already noticed the gradual societal drifts towards an over-concern with secondary life matters (particularly appearances), coupled with an exaggeration when displaying emotions; a 'superficialization' of life.

And this is ironic, because the purpose of our existence on Earth is to set our ranks in the Hereafter, and yet people's concern over earthly gains keeps them busy from attending to their Hereafter matters. Many people end up serving what was created to serve them (especially money), and get distracted from what they were primarily created for. The tools keep many people mesmerized from the task they were given the tools for! This is what God alerts us from:

They know what is apparent of the worldly life, but they, of the Hereafter, are unaware. [7] Do they not contemplate within themselves? Allah has not created the heavens and the earth and what is between them except in truth and for a specified term. And indeed, many of the people, in [the matter of] the meeting with their Lord, are disbelievers. [8] Have they not traveled through the earth and observed how was the end of those before them? They were greater than them in power, and they plowed the earth and built it up more than they have built it up, and their messengers came to them with clear evidences. And Allah would not ever have wronged them, but they were wronging themselves. [30: 7–9][1].

Many people engross themselves in this whirlpool despite the fact that God warned us from the temporary beauty of this life *'O mankind, fear your Lord and fear a Day when no father will avail his son, nor will a son avail his father at all. Indeed, the promise of Allah is truth, so let not the worldly life delude you and be not deceived about Allah by the Deceiver.'* [31: 33][1] ("the promise of Allah is truth" refers to the resurrection and judgment; "the Deceiver" refers to the devil). God gives us a similitude about this life we are in:

Know that the life of this world is but amusement and diversion and adornment and boasting to one another and competition in increase of wealth and children - like the example of a rain whose [resulting] plant growth pleases the tillers; then it dries and you see it turned yellow; then it becomes [scattered] debris. And in the Hereafter is severe punishment and forgiveness from Allah and approval. And what is the worldly life except the enjoyment of delusion. [57: 20][1].

The point being, although previous civilizations indulged themselves in pride due to the relative advancement and science they achieved, it did not avail them from God's wrath. This was explained to us in other verses:

Allah, it is He Who has made cattle for you, that you may ride on some of them and of some you eat. [79] And you have (many other) benefits from them, and that you may reach by their means a desire that is in your breasts (i.e. carry your goods, loads, etc.), and on them and on ships you are carried. [80] And He shows you His Signs and Proofs (of His Oneness in all the above mentioned things). Which, then of the Signs and Proofs of Allah do you deny? [81] Have they not travelled through the earth and seen what was the end of those before them? They were more numerous than them and mightier in strength, and in the traces (they have left behind them) in the land, yet all that they used to earn availed them not. [82] Then when their Messengers came to them with clear proofs, they were glad (and proud) with that which they had of

*the knowledge (of worldly things): And that at which they used to mock,
surrounded them (i.e. the punishment). [40: 79–83]*[2].

Finally, God presents to disbelievers a tangible challenge which, if they accomplished, would demonstrate that they are capable of deterring their transition into the phases of judgment, and hence there would definitely be no judgement day. God challenges them saying:

Is it such a talk (this Quran) that you (disbelievers) deny? [81] And instead (of thanking Allah) for the provision He gives you, on the contrary, you deny Him (by disbelief)! [82] Then why do you not (intervene) when (the soul of a dying person) reaches the throat? [83] And you at the moment are looking on, [84] But We (i.e. Our angels who take the soul) are nearer to him than you, but you see not, [85] Then why do you not, if you are exempt from the reckoning and recompense (punishment, etc.) [86] Bring back the soul (to its body), if you are truthful? [56: 81–87][2].

Still yet, some disbelievers persisted in their stubbornness, using the argument that if Muhammad's (may Allah bless him and grant him peace) statement that resurrection is true, it should be proven to them by resurrecting their fathers so they can see them. Those people are ignorant of the fact that God already decreed a specific time whence everyone will be resurrected in one instant (which only He knows when), and it is God's will (word) that has prevalence over theirs.

It's not for them to wish when to resurrect their fathers, nor is it their right to challenge God. Some have a misconception that believing in God will benefit Him in some way, but God doesn't need their believing in Him, for God is far greater than for people to benefit Him by worshipping Him.

So it is never a favour to God that a person believes in Him. On the contrary, it is a favour from God on an individual that He showed and led him to the path of truth. This is what God ordered Muhammad (may Allah bless him and grant him peace) to say to those who behaved and spoke to him like it was a grace from them to believe and follow him into Islam *'They regard as favour upon you (O Muhammad SAW) that they have embraced Islam. Say: "Count not your Islam as a favour upon me. Nay, but Allah has conferred a favour upon you, that He has guided you to the Faith, if you indeed are true"* [49: 17][2].

In a moment of self-honesty, one will realize that disbelieving in God is ungratefulness

Those who believe in God may ask themselves a very troublesome question: why is the punishment so severe (to burn in Hell eternally) for those who disbelieve? The truth is, those who disbelieve in God are denying Him what is rightfully His, which is the right to be obeyed (and hence worshipped) and the right to be thanked (praised) for all the blessings He bestowed upon them. It goes without saying, a disbeliever fulfils neither.

Firstly, a person should consider two aspects that need to be established. The first of which is making justice prevail, and that is achieved by giving everyone his right, including people's rights from each other.

The second is maintaining order, for if disbelievers weren't so severely punished, then even the believers would casually sin to maximize their enjoyment, in an attempt to enjoy life on Earth and in the Hereafter too, after getting a slap on the wrist. Bearing in mind these two aspects, it becomes understandable how eternal punishment is rightfully deserved by the disbeliever. Here is what God says about men who disbelieve, and hence defy Him, in spite of all that He has blessed them with:

Cursed is man; how disbelieving is he. [17] From what substance did He create him? [18] From a sperm-drop He created him and destined for him; [19] Then He eased the way for him; [20] Then He causes his death and provides a grave for him. [21] Then when He wills, He will resurrect him. [22] No! Man has not yet accomplished what He commanded him. [23] Then let mankind look at his food – [24] How We poured down water in torrents, [25] Then We broke open the earth, splitting [it with sprouts], [26] And caused to grow within it grain [27]

And grapes and herbage [28] And olive and palm trees [29] And gardens of dense shrubbery [30] And fruit and grass – [31] [As] enjoyment for you and your grazing livestock. [80: 17–32][1].

With these verses, it is clearer why disbelievers will be punished so severely. It is for consuming all those blessings whilst being too arrogant and proud to do a very simple thing: admit that there is just one God who gave them all this. And God emphasizes upon this fact, confronting man with an inquisition *'O mankind, what has deceived you concerning your Lord, the Generous, [6] Who created you, proportioned you, and balanced you? [7] In whatever form He willed has He assembled you'* [82: 6–8][1].

Their status is especially dire considering that man passes by multiple signs in nature indicating the existence of God, yet disbelievers are indifferent towards them. One such sign is this:

Do they not see that We have created for them from what Our hands have made, grazing livestock, and [then] they are their owners? [71] And We have tamed them for them, so some of them they ride, and some of them they eat. [72] And for them therein are [other] benefits and drinks, so will they not be grateful? [36: 71–73][1].

Isn't it peculiar how the creatures that have great benefit for man (having edible meat, are suitable for transport, produce milk, etc.) are easily tamed, and are afraid of attacking humans although they are larger and stronger? Even if they attack a human, their attacks are non-lethal, so they are generally safe. There are creatures which are smaller than cattle, such as wolves, which are disloyal, dangerous, and are not beneficial to man.

Can it be coincidental to this degree that, generally, useful animals to mankind are extremely passive. This difference in animal instincts actually has a noticeable pattern, indicating that it is intended to be so.

On another issue, there is an aspect that many people overlook, which is that God decrees upon His worshippers to treat the unfortunate well just as He bestowed His blessings generally upon people. For example, there is a commandment stating that a person is required to give out charity yearly, set at 2.5% of his savings, provided that he exceeded a specified value of savings (the equivalent of 85 grams of gold) throughout that period.

However, a lot of disbelievers don't exercise charity duly because they don't consider the needy sufficiently, or may overlook the benefits of giving charity. Others may expediently resort to a paradox to avoid donating to the poor from their savings: *'And when it is said to them, "Spend from that which Allah has provided for you," those who disbelieve say to those who believe, "Should we feed one whom, if Allah had willed, He would have fed? You are not but in clear error."* [36: 47][1]. Some others may go as far as mock, bully or speak disdainfully to the poor.

Alas, such individuals are oblivious to the fact that this difference in wealth distribution, which God intentionally caused, is a test for both the rich and the poor. He had informed us about this, but many people are ignorant of this knowledge *'And it is He who has made you successors upon the earth and has raised some of you above others in degrees [of rank] that He may try you through what He has given you. Indeed, your Lord is swift in penalty; but indeed, He is Forgiving and Merciful.'* [6: 165][1].

The test is to see whether the rich will mercifully assist the poor from their personal money or not; and whether the poor will be patient or will resort to immoral means to obtain money. Some poor people see that due to the 'unfair' hand that they have been dealt in life, this justifies stealing. Meanwhile, some rich people attribute their wealth to their personal efforts and intelligence, and so refrain from charity.

They refrain on grounds such as that poor people aren't skilful enough, need to put more effort, or will misuse that charity. However, they likely have not pondered upon themselves: how did they get these healthy bodies and intelligent minds? If wealth was based on such personal aspects and not on God's blessings, then how come there are people who are more intelligent and work harder than them yet still remain average in wealth or even poor?

The fact of the matter is that wealth is a result of other inherited blessings, and thus just another blessing from God, just as health, beauty and intelligence are basically inherited blessings. God chooses what combination of such blessings to bestow upon whom. *'Do they not know that Allah extends provision for whom He wills and restricts [it]? Indeed in that are signs for a people who believe.'* [39: 52][1].

And of the disbelievers who do give out charity, the result it is not wholly as efficient because they don't carry it out in an organized method. Upon such, God condemns those who abstain from such humane matters saying:

Nay! But you treat not the orphans with kindness and generosity (i.e. you neither treat them well, nor give them their exact right of inheritance)! [17] And urge not on the feeding of AlMiskin (the poor)! [18] And you devour inheritance all with greed, [19] And you love wealth with much love! [20] Nay! When the earth is ground to powder, [21] And your Lord comes with the angels in rows, [22] And Hell will be brought near that Day. On that Day will man remember, but how will that remembrance (then) avail him? [23] He will say: "Alas! Would that I had sent forth (good deeds) for (this) my life!" [89: 17–24][2].

If we notice, God followed His condemnation of those who treat the needy neglectfully with the catastrophes on the Day of Judgment. This indicates how significant it is to God that people help the needy, and that those who do not alleviate the suffering of the needy deserve to be warned, and ultimately punished if they ignore the warnings. And why shouldn't God warn them from such a day, for it is no small matter when the disbeliever sees how God's power overwhelms the angels (who are far greater than us in strength and complexity of creation) to such an extent that He makes them stand in organized rows!

Even further, there are disbelievers who still await more good fortune after all of what they are doing. How can they be convinced that the blessings they are receiving from God, in spite of their defiance of Him and preventing good from reaching people (or even harming them), is good fortune to them? They aren't paying back for what they are accumulating, and God warns them about that *'Do they think that what We extend to them of wealth and children [55] Is [because] We hasten for them good things? Rather, they do not perceive.'* [23: 55–56][1].

Some disbelievers may also speculate over God's actions, suggesting that if God did exist He would've done so and so instead of such. These speculations involve divine matters, such as the distribution of blessings between people, seeing that God would prioritize blessing people with a high status rather than those who are unfortunate. Practically, this thereby makes blessings confined to those who are already fortunate. The result of that scenario would be that the rich would get richer while the unfortunate gets ignored or even stepped upon.

As an example in the Quran, some saw that the Quran was supposed to be revealed to a man with great wealth and status amongst them, instead of being revealed to Prophet Muhammad (may Allah bless him and grant him peace), who was an illiterate orphan. They claimed that if it had been revealed to an elite person from amongst them, they would have believed the Quran and followed it.

But God rebukes them, questioning them about the multiple rights they are violating, for it is neither their blessings to bestow nor are they in need of more blessings. Furthermore, they don't have the required knowledge, wisdom and insight to deduce who is the most deserving of it.

Do they distribute the mercy of your Lord? It is We who have apportioned among them their livelihood in the life of this world and have raised some of them above others in degrees [of rank] that they may make use of one another for service. But the mercy of your Lord is better than whatever they accumulate. [43: 32][1].

So I ask the reader, how is it fair that those who arrogantly and hard-headedly disbelieved in Hell not be made to enter what they so assertively denied its existence? Why should disbelievers who spent their whole life using (and even abusing) God's blessings upon them, whilst denying that He gave it to them, be exempted from the accountabilities of their wilful decision to disbelieve in God? They, as God expressed, returned His blessings upon them with defiance and corruptive actions *'Have you not considered those who exchanged the favor of Allah for disbelief and settled their people [in] the home of ruin?'* [14: 28][1].

Why should they be exempt from the severe torment, especially that some of them had realized, but concealed, within themselves that there are signs truly indicating the existence of God? They know it and God knows it, yet they defiantly chose to maintain their stance and deny the signs of His existence. *'And they rejected them, while their [inner] selves were convinced thereof, out of injustice and haughtiness. So see how was the end of the corrupters.'* [27: 14][1].

They spent their finite lives on the sin of denying God His rights, but in proportionality to their life span, they infinitely defied God arrogantly. Doesn't doing this deserve infinite lasting punishment, especially when just admitting that there is one God (i.e. without performing any physical religious duties even) would have cost them nothing?

The repercussions of disbelieving in God on this world

Let's set aside the punishment that is promised to the disbeliever in the Hereafter and let's address the tangible aspects of this on Earth. The reality is that what keeps a person upholding his morals is his hatred of the consequences of not abiding by them. The consequence may be a nagging conscience, retribution by law such as a fine or prison, or the censure from people and their distancing from him.

One of the most effective factors that keep people in line is the certainty of punishment, which is proven by the fact that crime rates increase when people are absolutely certain they will not be caught. So on a higher scale, what keeps people from doing the wrong thing when no one is watching, when they are by themselves? The answer is: their certainty that there is someone watching them all the time, who will judge and recompense them (God). If this factor is eliminated, how do we expect people to abide by morale most of the time?

In other words, what is the consequence if they violate their morals? If the answer is: nothing, then the doors of corruption have been opened to them. And that is the point that God directs us towards, that how can it be expected from those that disbelieve in judgment day to abide by the righteous morals rather than their own set of morals. Personal morals, which vary from person to person, almost always have a fatal error, like that who doesn't condemn adultery, whilst another doesn't condemn lying, and so on.

This is directed to us in the question '*Then how can you fear, if you disbelieve, a Day that will make the children white-haired?*' [73: 17][1]. How will a person truly be virtuous and avoid wrongdoing after disbelieving in God and, subsequently, a horrendous day in which he will receive payback for his crimes? God emphasizes this with an example of a man who cheats people out of their goods during trading.

Woe to the defrauders, [1] Who, when they take the measure (of their dues) from men take it fully, [2] But when they measure out to others or weigh out for them, they are deficient. [3] Do not these think that they shall be raised again [4] For a mighty day, [5] The day on which men shall stand before the Lord of the worlds? [83: 1–6][6].

The factor of fear from retribution, which is one of the powerful restrictive factors to a person's misbehaviour, is greatly reduced regarding a disbeliever. Therefore, this individual is more likely to commit wrong, no matter how much he may argue that it is not true.

This is logically expected, for what will prevent a disbeliever from wrongdoing when he desires to do it whilst knowing there will be no punishment for it? And this is proven by the fact that there is a fairly common concept adopted and promoted within disbelievers: enjoy life to the fullest. This concept is embodied in mottos such as: YOLO (you only live once).

And God faces us with this fact, that it our nature to want to fulfil all our desires without restrictions, which encourages disbelieving in Judgment Day to remove one's limits. But if everyone just fulfils all of his desires and does whatever he pleases, the world would fall into anarchy, which is not the path that God has set for us. So some of us believe in God and restrain themselves from detrimental desires, whilst others keep disbelieving. God questions the latter group:

Does man think that We will not assemble his bones? [3] Yes. [We are] Able [even] to proportion his fingertips. [4] But man desires to continue in sin. [5] He asks, "When is the Day of Resurrection?" [6] So when vision is dazzled [7] And the moon darkens [8] And the sun and the moon are joined, [9] Man will say on that Day, "Where is the [place of] escape?" [10] No! There is no refuge. [11] To your Lord, that Day, is the [place of] permanence. [12] Man will be informed that Day of what he sent ahead and kept back. [13] Rather, man, against himself, will be a witness, [14] Even if he presents his excuses. [75: 3–15][1] ("sent ahead and kept back" refers to man's deeds, the evil of which he sent to his Hereafter, and the good of which he postponed and forgot to do, thereby not sending it to aid himself).

So we, as a race, are dependent on God's judgmental system so that our lives can be ordered, just as how (on a smaller scale) we need the law to be enforced upon criminals to maintain order in the community. Therefore, practically, whoever disregards God's guidance will inevitably cause overall corruption on Earth even if he does some benefit to people.

And this is what God foreknowingly invokes us to face ourselves with, saying '*Then, in case you turn away, might it be that you corrupt in the earth and sever your bonds of kin?*' *[47: 22]*[2]. The emphasis on cutting a person's bonds to his parents, siblings and relatives depicts how much corruption this causes on Earth, but many individuals do not perceive this.

Another example of corruption is gathering as much money as a person can for himself whilst withholding it from other people, which frequently reaches the point of extravagance. This stems from greed and the fear of falling into a financial crisis. God informs us of our untamed nature *'Say (to the disbelievers): "If you possessed the treasure of the Mercy of my Lord (wealth, money, provision, etc.), then you would surely hold back (from spending) for fear of (being exhausted), and man is ever miserly!"* [17: 100][2].

Upon this issue, there are verses in the Quran that draw our attention to a very peculiar phenomenon, which is that certain characteristics are more frequently found in those who disbelieve in God. Such characteristics are: *'Have you seen him who denies the Recompense? [1] That is he who repulses the orphan (harshly), [2] And urges not the feeding of AlMiskin (the poor),'* [107: 1–3][2]. Such verses carry a secondary message, that believing in God tends to drive individuals into amending the negative characteristics inherent in human nature, such as greed.

A related repercussion, regarding morality, is the loss of a reliable source to learn right from wrong in the first place. Whomever doesn't believe in God consequently doesn't believe in a Holy book sent from Him, and hence does not follow it. One of the aspects that a Holy book handles is morality, providing humans with a comprehensive list on what is right and what is wrong, based on ultimate knowledge and wisdom.

Since a disbeliever will not follow these codes, he is left with learning morality mainly through trial and error, and through advice also but to a lesser extent. This is a dilemma, because with this method he will tend to make more faults, harming himself and those around him in his learning process.

This point is one which God draws our attention to through a similitude, contrasting the state of a man walking on a ragged path and falls on his face frequently against a man who walks balanced on a paved path. God says *'Then is one who walks fallen on his face better guided or one who walks erect on a straight path?'* [67: 22][1]. This does not mean that a disbeliever will definitely be an immoral person, it means that he will take more time to know the righteous morals.

Furthermore, he will never be right on all the moral issues although he may be keen on being moral, due to deductive errors. People's views and desires differ, and thus their rules differ, so they can never reach an undisputable agreement upon what is immoral or immoral upon all matters. On the other hand, those who follow the Holy book from God are educated and trained about what is right and what is wrong. The result is that they have a unified reference regarding morality, and tend to fall less into errors or evil when they encounter them for the first time.

This situation is very similar to the educational system. Those who graduate from school know how to do advanced math, understand how nature functions, know how to utilize the laws of physics in day to day situations, etc. When both an educated person and an uneducated person encounter a mental challenge in life, the educated person is much more likely to avoid errors and overcome it first. Organized learning, which is based on a good syllabus and bound to a time frame, is always more fruitful, effective and efficient than unorganized learning.

As a conclusion to this section, I propose to every atheist a very logical argument based upon a hypothesis given to us in the Quran, *'And indeed, we or you are either upon guidance or in clear error'* [34: 24][1]. So essentially, one of us is right and the other is wrong concerning the presence of God.

Therefore, there MUST be a risk that one of us is taking. But it isn't in believing because if there is no God (although we are certain without a shred of doubt that He exists), then we lose nothing overall since all humans will meet the same fate: death and the wiping of memories. The ultimate perishing of all lives yields the same result regardless of the hardship of the path taken: pointlessness. However, if you are wrong, you cannot under any presumption get convinced that you will emerge from this victorious by entering Heaven, even if you spent life doing a lot of beneficial things to humanity.

There is a verse in the Quran dealing with this specific issue, by reflecting it upon a specific incident. The pagan Arabs used to fight the concept of the one and only God, whilst on the other hand they used to feed and alleviate the burden upon pilgrims who came from all around the globe for worship. Furthermore, they used to tend to the upkeep of the Kaaba in Mecca (which is the sacred pilgrim site), since they were the ones in charge of it at that period. The verse states:

Have you made the providing of water for the pilgrim and the maintenance of al-Masjid al-Haram equal to [the deeds of] one who believes in Allah and the Last Day and strives in the cause of Allah? They are not equal in the sight of Allah. And Allah does not guide the wrongdoing people. [9: 19][1].

Thus it was made clear, that this very honourable deed of aiding the pilgrims and tending to the Sacred Mosque does not match believing in the one and only God. God rejects counting it as a good deed for them since they don't acknowledge Him as the sole supervisor and judger of deeds in the first place.

Moreover, in conjunction with those great deeds, they cause grave corruption in the land resulting from ignoring God's regulatory rules. This corruption they cause practically turns out to be greater than the benefit they do when calculated. So, is a person who lives a boundary-free life equal to someone who strives to obey God and is keen in establishing righteousness in the land?

1.2 Partners with God!?

To sanctify anything to the degree of being convinced it deserves to be worshiped necessitates that this entity has earned the right to be worshipped. And so, adding a partner to God in worship is the greatest injustice to ever be done. This is because the individual then attributes what he does not own in the first place (the initiation, ownership and power over all creation) to someone who has no right in it nor is able to maintain it.

Since this injustice is done on a divine level and regarding such an immense matter (the ownership of the Heavens and Earth), there is no injustice whatsoever graver than this. So a person must assess the situation logically to avoid going astray.

The logical question

The frank question that we should ask ourselves and figure out through reason and experience, is a question that the messenger Joseph (may Allah grant him peace) asked his fellow prison-mates when he was unjustly imprisoned. The question he asked them was:

"O my two companions of the prison! (I ask you): are many lords differing among themselves better, or the One Allah, Supreme and Irresistible? [39] "If not Him, ye worship nothing but names which ye have named, ye and your fathers, for which Allah hath sent down no authority; the command is for none but Allah, He hath commanded that ye worship none but Him, that is the right religion, but most men understand not... [12: 39–40][2].

Joseph (may Allah grant him peace) asks whether the Universe would be more synchronized if there is only one God or would it run more efficiently if it had multiple God's controlling it. Even to us on a much smaller scale, we know that any company has one leading position (head executive or manager), so only one person runs the company. Having more than one leader will cause disorder and bring the company down. Due to this matter in general, there is a saying: too many cooks spoil the broth.

Moreover, if we were to speak of the emotional side in addition to the logical aspect, it is of human instinct that he feels much more rightful and more serene when he directs all his worship and prayers to the one God. On the other hand, praying to a variety of Gods makes the person unsettled and disarrayed. In addition, he is more likely to disbelieve in the presence of a God altogether because of the unexplainable aspects and contradictions he sees and feels when believing in multiple Gods.

If there were partners with God, they would quarrel for control.

It is way above our capacity to think of such matters in detail. However, God has brought the general concept under light in order to annul any excuses for associating partners with Him. God said '*Say, [O Muhammad], "If there had been with Him [other] gods, as they say, then they [each] would have sought to the Owner of the Throne a way." [42] Exalted is He and high above what they say by great sublimity*' [17: 42–43][1].

And that is a very logical matter that we ourselves witness similarly in our lives. Any major company operates with only one head manager (the chief executive officer, CEO) who is in charge and responsible of everything. This CEO position is what everyone else in the company aspires to, no matter how small the company is, they strive for it.

Some do so by resorting to immoral means even, such as falsely tarnishing the current CEO's reputation, or by setting up a problem for him so that he fails and ultimately loses his position. This regarding a company of limited influence, so how strong will the desire be to reach (and subsequently, the intensity of the clashes become) regarding a position of ownership and control over this entire Universe!?

Undoubtedly, if there were partners with the owner of The Throne (God), they would all compete with Him over this position of authority. Thus it would have been an everlasting struggle. So the ultimate fact is, there is but one God to this Universe. And there is no deity below Him, because God does not allow intermediaries between Himself and His slaves, He wills that all their worship and pleas to be communicated directly to Him.

If more than one God ruled this entire universe, it would collapse

In the previous section we discussed how the presence of associates with God will cause them to become greedy and strive to take His position. But we also need to ask ourselves: what are the consequences of this struggle? We could return to the example of a company as a representation, but the condition of a country is a clearer example.

Consider a country that undergoes successive coups. A country that is torn with turmoil from within via civil wars and constant overthrows, with its populace busy fighting over position of president, how can it be a prosperous and advanced nation? How when it is eating within itself and busy directing its resources to the struggle instead of advancing itself?

How will it give its citizens their rights and tend to their needs when it is an unstable country, and the presidents themselves are running after their own gains at the expense of the citizen's lives? Moreover, the president in this country keeps changing, and every president has different goals and different strategies in running the country. So with every change in president, there would be a change in the country's system, each demolishing what his predecessor did so that he can build differently. And to those who know how companies run, what do they think about a company who changes its policies and system very frequently; is it an efficient company or does that affect the company and weaken it?

The same is for this Universe, if there are partners struggling for God's authority, would it have been a stable and synchronized Universe? Definitely not, it would have fallen into chaos and collapsed. So that was in regards to the assumption that there are multiple gods whilst only one is ruling, however, there is another obsolete assumption that some polytheists hypothesize. They presume that there are multiple gods ruling the universe at the same time.

For that argument, God annuls saying '*Allah has not taken any son, nor has there ever been with Him any deity. [If there had been], then each deity would have taken what it created, and some of them would have sought to overcome others. Exalted is Allah above what they describe [concerning Him]*' [23: 91][1]. In this assumption, every god would have influence over an aspect in the Universe by himself (for example, one controls the sun and another controls the moon), resulting in that every god would do as he wishes with what he has control over.

Surely, this would lead to incoordination (between the sun and moon), so imagine the impact on us when day and night aren't regular and have variable durations each day. Moreover, it is very likely that the sun and moon would eventually collide, and clashes would ensue between the gods. Ultimately, this will lead to the fall of this universe into chaos with the perishing of all life forms, since it would be impossible to thrive in such a fluctuating and harsh environment. Even inanimate structures would perish as well, such as the planets and stars.

If there was more than one God ruling this universe, the best case scenario that could be expected is that the Universe would be disordered at the very least. '*Or have they chosen gods from the earth who raise the dead? [21] If there were therein gods beside Allah, then verily both (the heavens and the earth) had been disordered. Glorified be Allah, the Lord of the Throne, from all that they ascribe (unto Him)*' [21: 21–22][4]. But, thankfully to God, the reality is that we do not find any gaps or malfunctions in the system of the Universe, in spite of its vastness and complexity.

What power do these associated things have?

God gently and logically draws the attention of those that worship others with Him, by telling Prophet Muhammad (may Allah bless him and grant him peace) to ask them to look at the basic facts. It comes:

Say "Who provides for you from the heaven and the earth? Or who controls hearing and sight and who brings the living out of the dead and brings the dead out of the living and who arranges [every] matter?" They will say, "Allah," so say, "Then will you not fear Him?" [31] For that is Allah, your Lord, the Truth. And what can be beyond truth except error? So how are you averted? [32] Thus the word of your Lord has come into effect upon those who defiantly disobeyed - that they will not believe. [33] Say, "Are there of your 'partners' any who begins creation and then repeats it?" Say, "Allah begins creation and then repeats it, so how are you deluded?" [34] Say, "Are there of your 'partners' any who guides to the truth?" Say, "Allah guides to the truth. So is He who guides to the truth more worthy to be followed or he who guides not unless he is guided? Then what is [wrong] with you - how do you judge?" [35] And most of them follow not except assumption. Indeed, assumption avails not against the truth at all. Indeed, Allah is Knowing of what they do [10: 31–36][1].

A question over a more advanced matter was asked: what have those associated things created? God says:

Say "Who is The Lord of the heavens and the earth?" Say "Allah." Say "Then have you taken to yourselves, apart from Him, constant patrons (who) do not possess for themselves neither profit nor harm?" Say "Are the blind (man) and the beholding (one) equal? Or even are the darknesses and the light equal?" Or have they made up for Allah associates who created the like of His creation, so that creation appeared similar to them? Say "Allah is The Creator of everything and He is The One, The Superb Vanquisher." [13: 16][2].

If we look around us, we see breath-taking creation that is beautiful, sound in basis (i.e. functionally), flawless (e.g. no fissures in the sky or in the seas), and furthermore synchronized with the multitude of other created entities. God tells us to reflect upon His creation informing us:

He created the heavens without pillars that you see and has cast into the earth firmly set mountains, lest it should shift with you, and dispersed therein from every creature. And We sent down rain from the sky and made grow therein [plants] of every noble kind. [10] This is the creation of Allah. So show Me what those other than Him have created. Rather, the wrongdoers are in clear error. [31: 10–11][1].

Another matter that was questioned is the associated partners' ability in monitoring and maintaining all the creation, for God feeds, guides and protects those whom He wills to. That is in addition to the fact that He sees and hears (and knows the secret thoughts of) everyone at the same time, monitoring them to judge and recompense them upon their deeds. So which of the associates are similar to Him? God questions:

Then is He who is a maintainer of every soul, [knowing] what it has earned, [like any other]? But to Allah they have attributed partners. Say, "Name them. Or do you inform Him of that which He knows not upon the earth or of what is apparent of speech?" Rather, their [own] plan has been made attractive to those who disbelieve, and they have been averted from the way. And whomever Allah leaves astray - there will be for him no guide. [13: 33][1].

So how can anyone level between something that cannot create anything, and God who created everything *'Then is He who creates like one who does not create? So will you not be reminded?' [16: 17][1].* And God denounces this habit of equalling incompetent associates to Him and subsequently worshiping them:

And they worship besides Allah that which does not possess for them [the power of] provision from the heavens and the earth at all, and [in fact], they are unable [73] So do not assert similarities to Allah. Indeed, Allah knows and you do not know. [74] Allah presents an example: a slave [who is] owned and unable to do a thing and he to whom We have provided from Us good provision, so he spends from it secretly and publicly. Can they be equal? Praise to Allah! But most of them do not know. [75] And Allah presents an example of two men, one of them dumb and unable to do a thing, while he is a burden to his guardian; wherever he directs him, he brings no good. Is he equal to one who commands justice, while he is on a straight path? [76] And to Allah belongs the unseen [aspects] of the heavens and the earth. And the command for the Hour is not but as a glance of the eye or even nearer. Indeed, Allah is over all things competent. [16: 73–77][1].

He condemns it and gives two examples as to what idol worshippers are worshipping, to stress on the error in their belief. The first is a comparison between a slave who is incapacitated because he is bound to his master's wishes and between a free person who owns a lot of wealth and is able to do what he wants.

The second example is between a mentally challenged person who needs a guardian and can do no good, and a wise person who can lead people to the straight path. These two examples are similes to the difference in state between idols (who are handicapped and owned by God, since He created the raw materials they were manufactured from) and God.

So it is now understandable why God detests it when the beings He created worship others instead of Him, or worship others with Him. But on the other hand, it isn't just this fact. He also detests that mankind, whom He so much honoured (by making the Angels prostrate to their father Adam) and blessed with a mind to think with, would degrade themselves as to worship things that did not create the humans nor can benefit them! Additionally, many of the things that some humans worship are inferior to the humans themselves, so what kind of ignorance and self-humiliation is this?

Moreover, it is the human that carved those idols, so how is it logical that the human worships something he created by carving (from wood or stone) instead of worshipping who created him? And such aspects are what Prophet Ibrahim (peace be upon him) challenged the idols, and then his townsfolk, with:

Then he turned to their aliha (gods) and said: "Will you not eat (of the offering before you)? [91] "What is the matter with you that you speak not?" [92] Then he turned upon them, striking (them) with (his) right hand. [93] Then they (the worshippers of idols) came, towards him, hastening. [94] He said: "Worship you that which you (yourselves) carve? *[95] "While Allah has created you and what you make!" [37: 91–96]*[2].

God has honoured our father Adam (may Allah grant him peace) by ordering the Angels to prostrate to him, so is this what a human winds up doing, worshiping an inanimate statue or a human like him? Thus, the comprehensive question that God asks us is:

It is Allah Who has created you: further, He has provided for your sustenance; then He will cause you to die; and again He will give you life. Are there any of your (false) "Partners" who can do any single one of these things? Glory to Him! and high is He above the partners they attribute (to him)! [30: 40][2]. Thus, is there amongst those false deities anyone such?

And can these false deities deter off God's word upon someone whether it be punishment or mercy? *'Say, "Who is it that can protect you from Allah if He intends for you an ill or intends for you a mercy?" And they will not find for themselves besides Allah any protector or any helper'* [33: 17][1]. The truth is, these false deities cannot harm nor benefit themselves in any way, let alone those who worship them.

Furthermore, these associated things themselves seek survival from God's wrath and strive to gain His mercy, so how can anyone pray to them when these symbols are trying to find refuge for themselves from God? God said:

Say (O Muhammad SAW): "Call unto those besides Him whom you pretend [to be gods, like angels, Iesa (Jesus), 'Uzair (Ezra), etc.]. They have neither the power to remove the adversity from you nor even to shift it from you to another person." [56] Those whom they call upon [like 'Iesa (Jesus) - son of Maryam (Mary), 'Uzair (Ezra), angel, etc.] desire (for themselves) means of access to their Lord (Allah), as to which of them should be the nearest and they ['Iesa (Jesus), 'Uzair (Ezra), angels, etc.]

hope for His Mercy and fear His Torment. Verily, the Torment of your Lord is something to be afraid of! [17: 56–57][2].

And God invites us to rethink and ponder about who is in control of all that is around us in the Universe, asking a very logical question that shakes the very foundation of what we take for granted. He does so by asking:

Say, "Have you considered: if Allah should make for you the night continuous until the Day of Resurrection, what deity other than Allah could bring you light? Then will you not hear?" [71] Say, "Have you considered: if Allah should make for you the day (i.e. daylight) continuous until the Day of Resurrection, what deity other than Allah could bring you a night in which you may rest? Then will you not see?" [72] And out of His mercy He made for you the night and the day that you may rest therein and [by day] seek from His bounty and [that] perhaps you will be grateful. [28: 71–73][1].

It should be noted too, that with God's mercy of blessing us with day and night, He merges the day into the night gradually and the night into day gradually so that we don't get discomposed. God tells us:

Do you not see that Allah makes the night to enter into the day, and He makes the day to enter into the night, and He has made the sun and the moon subservient (to you); each pursues its course till an appointed time; and that Allah is Aware of what you do? [31: 29][6]. Imagine how disruptive it would be if the intense sunlight suddenly struck when the night was over, and darkness suddenly befell when daytime ended.

In the end, it must be pointed out how helpless these associated symbols are, and God has informed us as to how weak they are by giving us a new perspective. God asks us:

O mankind! A similitude has been coined, so listen to it (carefully): Verily! Those on whom you call besides Allah, cannot create (even) a fly, even though they combine together for the purpose. And if the fly snatched away a thing from them, they would have no power to release it from the fly. So weak are (both) the seeker and the sought. [73] They have not estimated Allah His Rightful Estimate; Verily, Allah is All-Strong, All-Mighty. [22: 73–74][2].

So if a fly, which is a relatively primitive creature compared to other creations from God, takes something (by engulfing it) from one of those associated symbols, those symbols cannot retrieve what the fly took from them. Furthermore, they are incompetent from creating just one fly even if they all combined their abilities, of which God had created countless more. This is regarding just one species of what God created.

And God points out that this is a simple request regarding a simple creature (the fly), and yet they are incapable of fulfilling it. This highlights how weak the seeker (the symbol that seeks retrieving what it owns from the fly) and the target sought (the fly). A seeker that is incapacitated when requested a simple task concerning a primitive creature, weaknesses over weaknesses; all are weak to Allah.

A core issue that leads people into associating partners with God is the ignorance of God's greatness. If a person starts to comprehend God's greatness, he would see how insignificant those false partners are, and would see how inappropriate it is to place them beside God in any aspect (fear, worship, reverence, etc.).

God said '*They have not appraised Allah with true appraisal, while the earth entirely will be [within] His grip on the Day of Resurrection, and the heavens will be folded in His right hand. Exalted is He and high above what they associate with Him.*' [43: 67][1]. This is why gaining reliable knowledge about God is a very important matter.

Who provides livelihood for living things?

When a person goes fishing, what is his guarantee that he will catch a fish? When a salesman opens his shop's door, when a taxi driver roams searching for a client, when a miner digs for gold, do any of them guarantee that he will gain a single earning? Does he know how much he will earn at the end of the day? This is especially evident in the first time for the fisherman, the salesman, the taxi driver, the miner; the thrill they all feel in their first catch or client or find is what proves they were dependent on an unpredictable factor.

The reality of the situation is that this factor is God's blessing; how much has God set for that person to receive as gains, and that is what the individual cannot know or guarantee. It is God that appointed for each person the quantity, method and timing of his earnings, for it is His Earth and His sky to provide for us from. This together with the fact that He is aware of every living thing He created, and has assigned unto Himself the provision for them all.

The point of mentioning all of this is: it is reasonable to demand, from whomever claims that blessings or livelihood come from someone, that proof be provided. In regards to God, He notified us in the Quran (with proof in it) that He provides for us our livelihood. Additionally, no person has contradicted this by claiming that it is he who provides livelihood for all living creatures.

Similarly, the same rule should be applied to any entity that is claimed to be a partner with God, in order to avoid deviating from the truth. An entity must be able to provide livelihood to all living creatures in order to deserve worship from them. God directs us *'Or, Who originates the creation, then reproduces it and Who gives you sustenance from the heaven and the earth. Is there a god With Allah? Say: Bring your proof if you are truthful.'* [27: 64][6].

What do these attributed partners to God have ownership of?

A very logical point that God guides us to ponder upon is: what do they own in the creations of the Earth and Heavens that compel a person to worship them? God asks admonishingly:

Say: "Have ye seen (these) 'Partners' of yours whom ye call upon besides Allah? Show Me what it is they have created in the (wide) earth. Or have they a share in the heavens? Or have We given them a Book from which they (can derive) clear (evidence)? Nay, the wrong-doers promise each other nothing but delusions. [35: 40][2].

And in another chapter, a similar rational question is asked. But this time, it is adjoined with a clarification of their absurd state, followed by a reminder of the consequence of turning a blind eye to God's advice. God ordered Prophet Muhammad (may Allah bless him and grant him peace) to say this to them:

Say, [O Muhammad], "Have you considered that which you invoke besides Allah? Show me what they have created of the earth; or did they have partnership in [creation of] the heavens? Bring me a scripture [revealed] before this or a [remaining] trace of knowledge, if you should be truthful." [4] And who is more astray than he who invokes besides Allah those who will not respond to him until the Day of Resurrection, and they, of their invocation, are unaware. [5] And when the people are gathered [that Day], they [who were invoked] will be enemies to them, and they will be deniers of their worship. [46: 4–6][1].

Thus, God incites the issue about who they attest to in ownership of the Universe, for they may reassess their actions and start to worship the creator alone. It comes:

Say: "To whom belong the earth and all beings therein? (say) if ye know!" [84] They will say, "To Allah!" say: "Yet will ye not receive admonition?" [85] Say: "Who is the Lord of the seven heavens, and the Lord of the Throne (of Glory) Supreme?" [86] They will say, "(They belong) to Allah." Say: "Will ye not then be filled with awe?" [87] Say: "Who is it in whose hands is the governance of all things,- who protects (all), but is not protected (of any)? (say) if ye know." [88] They will say, "(It belongs) to Allah." Say: "Then how are ye deluded?" [23: 84–89][2].

Upon this point, God advised His followers to use this fact as a logical argument against those who associate others with God. Why would a person worship something with God when it owns nothing, while God owns everything?

Say, "Is it other than Allah I should desire as a lord while He is the Lord of all things? And every soul earns not [blame] except against itself, and no bearer of burdens will bear the burden of another. Then to your Lord is your return, and He will inform you concerning that over which you used to differ." [6: 164][1].

One of the reasons that cause polytheists to create associates with God is the assumption that they are too small and insignificant to God to directly request from Him or ask for His forgiveness. Thus it ends up with them asking those symbols for forgiveness or even worshipping them, as a manner to please them so that the symbols would agree to intercede between them and God in commendation.

Setting aside that such a practice should be based upon evidence from scriptures from God, there still is a core issue which does not find a logical answer. The issue is: what do these symbols own that has any value to God, in order to have a stance with in front of God or to bargain over with? The reality is that they do not own anything precious to God in order to have a stance, nor are they infallible to reach the rank of being privileged with having a say in front of God.

Or have they taken other than Allah as intercessors? Say, "Even though they do not possess [power over] anything, nor do they reason?" [43] Say, "To Allah belongs [the right to allow] intercession entirely. To Him belongs the dominion of the heavens and the earth. Then to Him you will be returned." [39: 43–44][1].

Associating with God things that have flaws?

What is baffling to the mind is how some people associate with God, the Almighty who is all-complete, not only things that are powerless, but moreover have flaws too. How is it sensible to associate something with God that has flaws or weaknesses?

More importantly, how can something that has any flaw deserve to be worshipped in the first place, not to mention that some of these things are in fact inferior to those who are worshiping them? Such is the case when a person worships an idol, or even if he worships another human being because the target definitely has some feature flawed more than the worshiper.

God points out this to us in general, certain characteristics that denote a flaw in a worshipped thing, and yet some people ignore its presence. So He denounces this attitude questioningly:

Do they indeed ascribe to Him as partners things that can create nothing, but are themselves created? [191] No aid can they give them, nor can they aid themselves! [192] If ye call them to guidance, they will not obey: For you it is the same whether ye call them or ye hold your peace! [193] Verily those whom ye call upon besides Allah are servants like unto you: Call upon them, and let them listen to your prayer, if ye are (indeed) truthful! [194] Have they feet to walk with? Or hands to lay hold with? Or eyes to see with? Or ears to hear with? Say: "Call your 'god-partners', scheme (your worst) against me, and give me no respite! [195] "For my Protector is Allah, Who revealed the Book (from time to time), and He will choose and befriend the righteous. [196] "But those ye call upon besides Him, are unable to help you, and indeed to help themselves." [197] If thou callest them to guidance, they hear not. Thou wilt see them looking at thee, but they see not. [7: 191–198][2].

Who should people fear?

Since God has absolute power, authority and ability, He should be feared due to His wrath if invoked. At the same time, it is natural to love Him for the blessings He bestowed upon us. These are two opposing emotions that shouldn't coexist within a person towards anyone except God. So if God is to be feared, isn't it logical that a person shouldn't fear anyone that God didn't instruct us to fear? This is rational on the grounds that God the Almighty can protect His worshippers from anyone.

And that is what Prophet Ibrahim (may Allah grant him peace) deduced and used as an irrefutable argument with his kinsfolk, when he destroyed their idols and they warned him about their idols' vengeance. His irrefutable logical argument was '*And how should I fear what you associate while you do not fear that you have associated with Allah that for which He has not sent down to you any authority? So which of the two parties has more right to security, if you should know?'* [6: 81][1].

So he pointed out that they did not have any source as proof that God asked people to fear and worship those idols. And instead, it is them that should be the worried ones since they ascribed to Him things He did not authorize. This irrefutable logical argument was the same that Prophet Muhammad (may Allah bless him and grant him peace) faced polytheists with to open their eyes to the truth:

Or have they taken gods besides Him? Say, [O Muhammad], "Produce your proof. This [Qur'an] is the message for those with me and the message of those before me." But most of them do not know the truth, so they are turning away. [24] And We sent not before you any messenger except that We revealed to him that, "There is no deity except Me, so worship Me." [25] And they (wrongdoers) say, "The Most Merciful has taken a son." Exalted is He! Rather, they are [but] honored servants. [26] They cannot precede Him in word, and they act by His command. [27] He knows what is [presently] before them and what will be after them, and they cannot intercede except on behalf of one whom He approves. And they, from fear of Him, are apprehensive. [28] And whoever of them should say, "Indeed, I am a god besides Him"- that one We would recompense with Hell. Thus do We recompense the wrongdoers. [21: 24–29][1].

So the truth is, all the messengers who preceded Muhammad (may Allah bless them) came with the same core concept in their messages. They directed people to the fact that there is only one God, and to worship Him; whereas there is no definite proof that any of them directed people to worship anyone else (or themselves). That insinuation is the product of misleaders who distorted the meaning of some verses, deluding people to the lie that there are others that should be worshipped with God. Nowhere in any authentic Scripture did any messenger say: worship me.

And then God proceeds in describing and warning those who still insist on worshiping others besides Him, indicating that whoever claimed to be a God or encouraged people to worship himself shall be thrown in Hell. On the other hand, whoever people worshipped will disavow himself from his worshippers on judgment day in front of God from fear.

But since they cannot provide any tangible proof that God ordered them to worship anyone with Him, God condemns their insistence upon that path. Moreover, He represented their insistence as an attempt at telling God that these are His partners that He doesn't know about (thus pointing out its absurdity). God denounces their attitude saying:

They worship beside Allah that which neither hurteth them nor profiteth them, and they say: These are our intercessors with Allah. Say: Would ye inform Allah of (something) that He knoweth not in the heavens or in the earth? Praised be He and High Exalted above all that ye associate (with Him)! [10: 18][4].

So the overall point is: those who invented partners with God should present proof from Scriptures that God ordered people to associate them with Him. If they can't, then they are committing a grave crime and should fear God's wrath. They transferred what rightfully belongs to God alone unto others who don't deserve it (idols, humans, angels and so on), which is the right of worship. And logically speaking, if none of us refutes that God is Almighty and All-Owning, why would He include with Himself any partners to be worshipped with Him?

Jesus (may Allah grant him peace), a God?

It is a basic instinctive reasoning in humans to realize that a God is someone that is way superior to a human in terms of abilities. This means having absolute power, absolute authority, and exalted from any flaw however minuscule it may be, for He should be complete and absolute. The question is: did Jesus (may Allah grant him peace) have absolute power? If he did, then he would've prevented any harm from reaching him (especially the assumed crucifixion).

Moreover, if he was God, then he would've passed a law that all mankind should be exempt from their sins without the need for him to be crucified. He would have absolute authority and power to decree whatsoever he wishes without having to pass through the suffering.

Overall, it should be made clear that in Islam, we believe that Jesus (may Allah grant him peace) is not a God, he is a Prophet. And as a matter of fact, he is one of the most highly-regarded prophets from all the prophet chain, but nonetheless just a Prophet and not a God. God points out to us the facts that show he has the features attributable to a human and not a God:

The Messiah, son of Mary, was not but a messenger; [other] messengers have passed on before him. And his mother was a supporter of truth. They both used to eat food. Look how We make clear to them the signs; then look how they are deluded. [75] Say, "Do you worship besides Allah that which holds for you no [power of] harm or benefit while it is Allah who is the Hearing, the Knowing?" [76] Say, "O People of the Scripture, do not exceed limits in your religion beyond the truth and do not follow the inclinations of a people who had gone astray before and misled many and have strayed from the soundness of the way." [77] Cursed were those who disbelieved among the Children of Israel by the tongue of David and of Jesus, the son of Mary. That was because they disobeyed and [habitually] transgressed. [5: 75–78][1].

In explanation: "do not exceed limits in your religion beyond the truth" refers to taking Jesus Christ as a God, and creating unfounded rituals such as monasticism, with the forbidding of marriage and confinement to a monastery. "And do not follow the inclinations of a people who had gone astray before and misled many" refers to parents, leaders, and even scholars who have been found to have deviated from the path of the Scriptures.

So although Jesus (peace be upon him) was given some unique and astonishing miracles from God, such as resurrecting the dead, there are other Prophets who were also given miracles from God. For instance, Moses (may Allah grant him peace) had the miracle of his stick, alongside other miracles. Thus, possessing miracles does not mean he is a God, especially that he clearly advises us many times to worship God and never once requested to be worshiped himself.

Furthermore, God informs us in the Quran that Jesus (may Allah grant him peace) was never crucified, because he was so honoured by Him that He rescued him from the crucifixion. Instead, God made one of Jesus' followers to appear to them like Jesus (may Allah grant him peace), who in turn accepted to sacrifice himself in Jesus's place, and God lifted Jesus.

And so he hasn't died until this very moment because God preserved him (so he never died nor got resurrected yet), but right before judgment day, he will descend again. At that time, his descent is one of the major signs of judgment's day approximation as God informs us '*And indeed, Jesus will be [a sign for] knowledge of the Hour, so be not in doubt of it, and follow Me. This is a straight path*' [43: 61][1].

However, in spite of all this and how Jesus (may Allah grant him peace) is favoured by God, it is still very offensive to God when one of His creations (humans) claims that Jesus is God (or the son of God). That is because in this way, people ascribe God's power and His right of worship to someone other than Him, one who is merely a human.

Angels or demons related to God?

This is a very abominable proclamation, in that there is a relation between the angels and God. For example, the pagan Arabs claimed that angels were God's daughters, ironically in spite of the fact that they perceived females to be inferior to males.

Some factions even claim the angels are extensions of God. They do so although God has said this about the angels: '*But they have attributed to Him from His servants a portion. Indeed, man is clearly ungrateful. [15] Or has He taken, out of what He has created, daughters and chosen you for [having] sons?' [43: 15–16]*[1].

So how is it possible for His slaves, whom He created, to share with Him in the ownership of the Universe and hence deserve to be worshipped!? Moreover, they depicted angels as being female, which is apparent in the statues and drawings made. From where did this assumption arise and how did it flourish when God asks logically *'Or did We create the angels as females while they were witnesses?' [37: 150]*[1] (i.e. were those claimers alive and witnessed when God created the angels to claim that they are females?).

And some factions went even farther than this, like those who worship the devil (i.e. Jinn), claiming that there is a blood relationship between him and God! What a foul atrocity to be uttered. God said this about the Jinn *'And they imagine kinship between Him and the jinn, whereas the jinn know well that they will be brought before (Him)' [37: 158]*[4]. Even the Jinn themselves are certain that they will be made to stand in front of God for judgment on their actions, so how can they be related to God?

On a side note for clarification, Jinn are beings created from fire which we cannot see, while they can see us. They have a free will and thus can disobey God, like us. Consequently, some of them are good and some are bad (named devils), the most prominent of which is Satan. They should not be mixed with angels, who are beings created from light and are incapable of disobeying God; angels are a different entity from Jinn.

In the direst of situations, who does a person pray to?

In the most critical and bleakest of situations, when a person realizes that he is helpless in his disaster and nothing can assist him (especially if it is life threatening), he usually directs his prayers to the highest authority and power, which is God. The troubled person does not direct his prayers to the intermediary he placed between himself and God, that whom he associated with God.

People in their direst situations are so desperate that they plea their request to God directly, to the one who undoubtedly has the absolute power and absolute ability. That is because their situation cannot withstand any delay or mishandling from the beings they associate with God.

They do not want to submit their ultimately crucial matters to anyone other than God, due to the sensitive nature of their issue. They do not feel safe about handing their delicate issue to whom they associated with God, so is it logical that they worship who they can't completely trust?

And this is a fact that God points out to people through a logical question. If polytheists turn to God alone in the time of crisis, then why is it that when God resolves the problem or deflects the danger from them do they revert to worshipping the partners they attribute to God?

Say (O Muhammad SAW): "Tell me if Allah's Torment comes upon you, or the Hour (judgment day) comes upon you, would you then call upon any one other than Allah? (Reply) if you are truthful!" [40] Nay! To Him Alone you call, and, if He will, He would remove that (distress) for which you call upon Him, and you forget at that time whatever partners you joined with Him (in worship)! [6: 40–41][2]. And God gives us an example and directs us to think about it:

Say, "Who rescues you from the darknesses of the land and sea [when] you call upon Him imploring [aloud] and privately, 'If He should save us from this [crisis], we will surely be among the thankful.'" [63] Say, "It is Allah who saves you from it and from every distress; then you [still] associate others with Him." [6: 63–64][1].

And why would a person plea to God in dire situations and then change whom he pleas to if his request is responded to and his predicament passes? So the point is, how is it logical to pray to associated partners with God in times of welfare when in dire times people pray to God alone? Isn't it of integrity, loyalty and justice that the God we pray to at our times of distress be the same God we pray to at our times of ease? Or is the God that people endear different from the God they rely on!?

God warns from this attitude of man, of praying to Him at times of need but associating with Him at times of comfort, in that He may send His wrath upon them. So God questions them warningly: do they revert to that course (of associating with God) on grounds that they absolutely guarantee and feel absolutely safe that He will not send His torment?

And when distress afflicts you in the sea, away go those whom you call on except He; but when He brings you safe to the land, you turn aside; and man is ever ungrateful. [67] What! Do you then feel secure that He will not cause a tract of land to engulf you or send on you a tornado? Then you shall not find a protector for yourselves. [68] Or, do you feel secure that He will (not) take you back into it (the sea) another time, then send on you a fierce gale and thus drown you on account of your ungratefulness? Then you shall not find any aider against Us in the matter. [17: 67–69][6].

In the end, the fact remains, and that is '*Or, Who listens to the (soul) distressed when it calls on Him, and Who relieves its suffering, and makes you (mankind) inheritors of the earth? (Can there be another) god besides Allah? Little it is that ye heed!*' [27: 62][5]. So why argue with the truth?

1.3 Does God have a son?

Many factions have claimed that God has a son. Some Jews stated that Ezra is God's son, while some Christians stated that Jesus (may Allah grant him peace) is God's son, and ancient Arabs used to claim that the angels are God's daughters. Each faction believed that they are special to God because they follow (and worship) His children. This aroused suspicion by itself because of the different sons they attribute to God, in a situation in which they assert that they are building upon previous revelations. Each faction denied the other faction's symbol to be God's son whilst affirming their own symbol.

Why does God get offended when He is attributed a son?

First of all, it should be stated that attributing a son to God is an indirect claim that He has features comparable to that of a human (in that He wants to have a son), which is an undermining of His greatness. He is exalted from all such matters and exalted from being compared to a human's characteristics, for He is God.

Secondly, attributing a son to God means that someone has similar or near-like power and authority to Him, which is far from possible. It is Him alone who owns and controls every aspect of the universe.

Thirdly and fourthly, no one who believes in God denies that He is all-powerful and therefore does not need or rely on anyone/anything. A believer doesn't deny that God owns all that exists also. If they assert either of these features, then this belief cannot co-exist with a belief that He has a son. If He is all-powerful, it means He is self-sufficient and whole, which means He doesn't consist of segments or different natures; thus a fragment cannot be derived nor separate from Him – a son/daughter. It also means He does not need a child to aid or satisfy Him.

If He owns all that exists, it means that everything is a slave and should worship him. However, the feature of being a slave conflicts with the feature of being a son, since a son is not an item of ownership, rather it more closely resembles a copy of the father and is of the same nature. Thus, the claim of God having children violates reason, and moreover needs evidence.

They have said, "Allah has taken a son." Exalted is He; He is the [one] Free of need. To Him belongs whatever is in the heavens and whatever is in the earth. You have no authority for this [claim]. Do you say about Allah that which you do not know? [10: 68][1].

Lastly, when people attribute a son to God, they usually worship that 'son', thereby appointing someone (who has no right) to share with God the right of worship. And of course, it is God's right to be angry from those who direct their worship to others from the one who created them, Him.

God gives us a representation of such a person through Muhammad (may Allah bless him and grant him peace) who said while informing people of the five pillars of Islam: **The first of them is that you worship Allah and associate not anything with Him. And the example of one who associates with Allah is like a man who bought a slave with his pure earnings of gold or silver and said to him "This is my house and this is my business, so take up this occupation and pay me what you earn"; he works but pays another than his master. So, which of you will be pleased to have a slave like that?[7]**

That was a parable for us so that we would somewhat comprehend the absurdness of the situation. However, one can truly feel the calamity of that assertion and how much it offends God from the following verses:

And they say: The Beneficent Allah has taken (to Himself) a son. [88] Certainly you have made an abominable assertion [89] The heavens may almost be rent thereat, and the earth cleave asunder, and the mountains fall down in pieces, [90] That they ascribe a son to the Beneficent Allah. [91] And it is not worthy of the Beneficent Allah that He should take (to Himself) a son. [92] There is no one in the heavens and the earth but will come to the Beneficent Allah as a servant. [93] Certainly He has a comprehensive knowledge of them and He has numbered them a (comprehensive) numbering. [94] And every one of them will come to Him on the day of resurrection alone. [18: 88–95][6].

So that is the fact about the atrociousness of the situation. And logically speaking, how can anyone that is a servant to God and will be called upon individually for judgment have any power whatsoever or be God's son?

The truth concerning Jesus (may Allah grant him peace)

Jesus (may Allah grant him peace) in Christianity is currently believed to be either the son of God or God himself. However, the original Christians were certain that he was a Prophet from God, and as a matter of fact, very few of that faction still exist today. That was before the head scholars in Christianity collaborated and 'twisted' the meanings in the bible (by distorting the intended meaning of verses during translating/interpreting it), to imply that he is the son of God.

For example, the phrase "his only begotten son" [John 3: 16] in the King James Version of the bible was discovered to be an incorrect translation by successive Christian scholars. The word "begotten" was deemed an error, and thus removed. And such a distortion, undoubtedly intentional by some scholars, is in accordance with what God has enlightened us about in the Quran:

And indeed, there is among them a party who alter the Scripture with their tongues so you may think it is from the Scripture, but it is not from the Scripture, and they say "This is from Allah", but it is not from Allah. And they speak untruth about Allah while they know. [3: 78][1].

What is baffling is that it is too hard to imagine that head scholars, who are supposedly the trustees of the general populace, would do such a thing as collaborating to lie about God. Yet it happened. Nonetheless, for sceptics about this matter, this will be apparent if they review the historical origin of the trinity for example. Specifically worthy of mention is the debate of the ecumenical council of bishops in the year 325 AD, which was named: The First Council of Nicaea.

At this council, the (Nicene) creed of the trinity was established, and churches were expected to abide by it, which was later on enforced by the Roman's state law. Particularly prominent at that council was the eventual agreement that the Holy Spirit, who is actually the angel Gabriel that delivers God's message to messengers, is god-like. The Holy spirit was added to God in worship, after adding Jesus, thereby formulating the trinity. So a human and an angel were worshipped with God in actuality.

How could such fundamental matters be unknown before that time, and be subject to debate and establishment? This was illogical because what was established by this council meant that those worshipping God before that were worshiping God wrongly. How can the successors in a religion be more knowledgeable about a religion than the pioneers?

A thousand questions arise, like how did they establish this, why would they do this, and how can the majority of humans alive today possibly be adopting a wrongful belief? These questions aren't easy to find satisfactory answers to, which make this all hard to believe. But this is what a group of Jinn were shocked from when they heard the Quran and found it to be righteous, and so confessed after following it:

And (we believe) that He - exalted be the glory of our Lord! - hath taken neither wife nor son, [3] And that the foolish one among us used to speak concerning Allah an atrocious lie. [4] And lo! we had supposed that humankind and jinn would not speak a lie concerning Allah. [72: 3–5][4].

Yet the fact remains, millions of people believe that Jesus (may Allah grant him peace) is the son of God without definite proof of it, just the interpretive word of the priests. Subsequently, many keep arguing that this is the truth because they have been fed this concept all their life until they grew accustomed to it.

Ultimately, many people adopted it by dictation through generations and became attached to it, without comprehending, verifying, or analysing it logically. Many argue, out of arrogance, that God does have a son, as God informed us about them as he knows their secrets, since He created them:

And of the people is he who disputes about Allah without knowledge or guidance or an enlightening book [from Him], [8] Twisting his neck [in arrogance] to mislead [people] from the way of Allah. For him in the world is disgrace, and We will make him taste on the Day of Resurrection the punishment of the Burning Fire [while it is said] [9] 'That is for what your hands have put forth and because Allah is not ever unjust to [His] servants.' [22: 8–10][1].

The strange fact is that, even in the current translated versions of the Bible, it is not mentioned even once that Jesus himself said forthrightly: I am god. Neither did he ever say to people: worship me. On the contrary, he urges his followers to 'worship Him'.

Moreover, he says that he will return to his 'Father', an expression referring to God and not a literal meaning: *I am ascending to my Father and **your Father**, to my God and your God*' [John 20: 17]. The proof is that there is no Christian suggesting that God has other sons, nor that they are similar to Jesus (may Allah grant him peace) in terms of lineage to God.

So the verse is clearly specific, that father means God, and the reader is free to verify these facts. Nonetheless, current scholars justify the claim that Jesus (may Allah grant him peace) is God's son, indirectly, through subliminal meanings in certain verses. They practice this at a time where there are frank verses that prove otherwise. Why is there a need to resort to hidden meanings when there are clear verses informing us of the facts?

If he was in fact God or God's son, wouldn't he have made a clear statement of it, for it is not a matter that withstands ambiguity or controversy, since the consequences of a person erring is dire suffering. And after all, wasn't his goal to enlighten people with the truth, to clarify these fundamental issues to mankind and settle the controversy? Thus when the Quran was revealed to us, it was necessary to re-clarify this fact to all of humanity, and so God said:

This is what We recite to you, [O Muhammad], of [Our] verses and the precise [and wise] message [58] Indeed, the example of Jesus to Allah is like that of Adam. He created Him from dust; then He said to him, "Be," and he was [59] The truth is from your Lord, so do not be among the doubters [60] Then whoever argues with you about it after [this] knowledge has come to you - say, "Come, let us call our sons and your sons, our women and your women, ourselves and yourselves, then supplicate earnestly [together] and invoke the curse of Allah upon the liars [among us] [61] Indeed, this is the true narration, And there is no deity except Allah. And indeed, Allah is the Exalted in Might, the Wise [62] But if they turn away, then indeed - Allah is Knowing of the corrupters. [3: 58–63][1].

From these verses, we are given a sensible statement that Jesus (may Allah grant him peace) was created similarly to Adam (may Allah grant him peace), since everyone accepts how Adam was created without either parent. Then, God ordered Muhammad (may Allah bless him and grant him peace) to confront the Christians with this fact, since they secretly knew so from their original Scriptures but neglected it.

Muhammad (may Allah bless him and grant him peace) confronted them by offering a challenge that they all sit together (including their families) and pray to God for doom on the lying party, which the Christians back then refused. The Jews too refused a similar confrontational debate as will be mentioned later.

What is conclusive in determining the nature of Jesus (may Allah grant him peace) is his testimony about himself while he was an infant, when the townsfolk wondered about how the Virgin Mary begot a child. When they asked her about him, she did not reply but pointed to him instead to acquit her, and he started talking as stated in the Quran:

So she pointed to him. They said, "How can we speak to one who is in the cradle a child?" [29] [Jesus] said, "Indeed, I am the servant of Allah. He has given me the Scripture and made me a prophet. [30] And He has made me blessed wherever I am and has enjoined upon me prayer and zakah (i.e. charity) as long as I remain alive [31] And [made me] dutiful to my mother, and He has not made me a wretched tyrant. [32] And peace is on me the day I was born and the day I will die and the day I am raised alive." [33] That is Jesus, the son of Mary - the word of truth about which they are in dispute. [34] It is not [befitting] for Allah to take a son; exalted is He! When He decrees an affair, He only says to it, "Be," and it is. [35] [Jesus said], "And indeed, Allah is my Lord and your Lord, so worship Him. That is a straight path." [36] Then the factions differed [concerning Jesus] from among them, so woe to those who disbelieved - from the scene of a tremendous Day. [19: 29–37][1].

Jesus the Messiah (may Allah grant him peace) was conceived by the Virgin Mary by a command from God, sending His angel Gabriel to deliver her the news. But to whoever is still adamant on believing that Jesus is the son of God, God warns them and demonstrates His power by presenting them with a logical question:

In blasphemy indeed are those that say that Allah is Christ the son of Mary. Say: "Who then hath the least power against Allah, if His will were to destroy Christ the son of Mary, his mother, and all (every one) that is on the earth? For to Allah belongeth the dominion of the heavens and the earth, and all that is between. He createth what He pleaseth. For Allah hath power over all things." [5: 17][2].

Indeed, this is an important fact which God directs us towards. The fact is: do we think that Jesus can prevent God from exalting His power over him if He wills to make him perish?

Jesus is too virtuous to reject being a slave to God

This is a simple fact, that God is so powerful that every single creature sooner or later submits to the power of God and obeys Him, whether willingly (in life) or compulsively (in the Hereafter). And all natural entities have succumbed to God as He informs us *'Then He directed Himself to the heaven while it was smoke and said to it and to the earth "Come [into being], willingly or by compulsion." They said "We have come willingly."* [41: 11][1]. Only humans and Jinn were left out, who split up into those that submitted to God in this life whilst the rest will undoubtedly succumb to His power in the Hereafter.

And Jesus (may Allah grant him peace) was too wise and righteous to reject succumbing to the one and only God, the one who created him. God says about Jesus the Messiah *'Never would the Messiah disdain to be a servant of Allah, nor would the angels near [to Him]. And whoever disdains His worship and is arrogant - He will gather them to Himself all together'* [4: 172][1]. And that is the logical point, if God denies that Jesus (may Allah grant him peace) is His son and says he is but a slave, how could Jesus (may Allah grant him peace) dare to defy God's word by claiming that he is the son of God?

In summary to this chapter, by applying reason, some concepts in faith should be dismissed on account of illogicalness, namely that there is no God or that God has partners (including a son). By eliminating those concepts logically, only one rational deduction remains: that God is a single entity. This will be the basis on which the next chapters will build upon, starting by demonstrating that Islam is a religion that rightfully deserves consideration.

Islam is a religion whose doctrines revolve around the fundamental principle that there is just one God: Allah. This concept requires no added explanations or extended details; no complications. It is a monotheistic religion in the strictest sense. The concept regarding the presence of just one God does not accept any addition or subtraction; any modification would invalidate it. Upon this, we are ordered *'Say: He is Allah, the One! [1] Allah, the eternally Besought of all! [2] He begetteth not nor was begotten. [3] And there is none comparable unto Him.'* [112: 1–4][4].

Chapter 2: Verifying that Islam is a rightful religion

This chapter is aimed at proving that Islam is one of the religions that came from God, and that it is not a man-made or a void religion. We will start by eliminating the main assumption that it is not from God, which will be followed by refuting some of the accusations directed at Islam.

The ending section will conclude with definite proof that it is from God, by demonstrating that all the (technologically verifiable) scientific facts mentioned in the Quran have been confirmed experimentally or observationally. These scientific facts could not have been known in that historic era, yet not a single one of them turned out to be wrong. Concurrently, this means that this is a book from someone who is All-Knowledgeable without any doubt.

2.1 The denial that the Quran is from God

How can a person verify that the Quran is an authentic book from God? That is a very legitimate and critical question indeed, which is addressed below.

The ultimate fact

Any book authored by a human with detailed description on ideas and beliefs will contain some illogical or contradictory points, because the source of the book is a human, and humans themselves contain contradictions. Have we not seen the health-motivated athlete who smokes? Have we not seen a highly mannered person who commits adultery?

But, in contrast, a book that is sent to us from God will have no contradictions since God is the ultimate entity. The entity that is All-Knowing and All-Complete, free from any contradictions, flaws or weaknesses. Hence, the verification stamp of any book from God is that it is free from errors and contradictions within itself. This is fulfilled regarding the Quran. God directs people to a rational deduction '*Then do they not reflect upon the Qur'an? If it had been from [any] other than Allah, they would have found within it much contradiction*' [4: 82][1].

And that is the axiomatic fact, that the Quran has no contradictions because it comes from a higher entity than a human. However, many people claim to have found contradictions in the Quran, based on their biased desire to falsify this book, and apply various deceptive methods to support their claims.

Common methods include avoiding to quote the verses so that the reader cannot figure that there is no contradiction, or misinterpreting the verses. Misinterpretation causes the verse to give a different meaning than its actual meaning, which is carried out by taking it out of context for example, or implying that it refers to a person or event which it does not. This whilst deliberately ignoring authentic explanations of the Quranic verses.

Unjust disbelievers employ such tactics relying on the fact that their audience will not verify it after them, gambling that their audience will rather (out of easiness) accept their claims. They know that most of the audience will accept what they say out of good-will, and unlikely try to verify the facts personally by finding a copy of the Quran and reading the explanation of the verse.

So my advice to the reader is: if someone claims that there is a contradiction in the Quran, verify it yourself with the aid of an explication of the verses. Let your rationale and evaluation be the ones in charge of your destiny in the Hereafter. Be responsible of your own answers when you are standing alone facing your interrogation from God, and don't place yourself in a situation where your excuse lies on the words of another person. And God warned us from finding ourselves in such a predicament or a similar one.

He warns from trying to use the excuse that we were coerced by others to do injustice, or that we feared persecution from other people if we declared belief in Him, and remained disbelievers till death. This accompanied by the confession that it was not our intention to be so, just weakness from our part or by being victims. God said:

Indeed, those whom the angels take [in death] while wronging themselves - [the angels] will say "In what [condition] were you?", they will say "We were oppressed in the land." The angels will say, "Was not the earth of Allah spacious [enough] for you to emigrate therein?" For those, their refuge is Hell - and evil it is as a destination [4: 97][1].

And in that case, only those who were truly oppressed will be pardoned as God informs us (who had no means of escaping from the arrogant leaders, like old people), but God is the judge of that. So my fellow reader, do not let the motivations of others decide your fate in the Hereafter, which results from automatically trusting their allegations in this critical matter, and thus acting upon them. The reality is, some people will sell their own souls to gain fame, fortune or to uphold their false pride.

A simple test

God opens the door to disbelievers, suggesting to them a verification process that it is indeed His revelation:

And if you are in doubt about what We have sent down upon Our Servant [Muhammad], then produce a surah the like thereof and call upon your witnesses other than Allah, if you should be truthful [23] But if you do not -and you will never be able to- then fear the Fire, whose fuel is men and stones, prepared for the disbelievers. [2: 23–24][1].

In essence, God challenges disbelievers to gather whomever they want with them for assistance, and produce a surah (chapter) that is of the same calibre as one that is in the Quran. However, if they are incapable of doing so, then they should admit to the uniqueness of the Quran. This is, if they are sincere with God and themselves in their search and acceptance of the truth.

However, those that are unable to meet the challenge and yet resent believing deserve a warning about what awaits them. I personally encourage the sceptics to actually try to compose a few verses similar to the Quran in uniqueness, to comprehend the greatness in them. This will eliminate the deceiving assumption that doing so is easy. Only after accomplishing it can a person rightfully state whether it was easy or not.

And God already foretold us the result of this challenge, which is that all of mankind and Jinn are incapable of producing the like of it. This is the case since it is from a source of supreme knowledge and supreme power: God. *'Say, "If mankind and the jinn gathered in order to produce the like of this Qur'an, they could not produce the like of it, even if they were to each other assistants."* [17: 88][1].

What is peculiar to note is that this challenge was presented around 1400 years ago, and yet those who deny the divine source of the Quran continue to persistently argue in other issues, attempting to falsify the Quran. Why up till now has none of those arguers, within this 1400-year span, produced one chapter similar to the Quran to irrefutably prove his argument and decisively end this controversy?

By that he would have disproven something stated in the Quran and hence invalidated it, but many of them are beating around the bushes instead. Doesn't this behaviour incite wonder and suspicion, whilst asserting what is obvious?

A few stubborn individuals try to circle around this challenge by claiming that God has revealed a message unto them, and that they will present the message soon. Some even claim that they are messengers, but they rarely present any alleged scriptures, and if they do, it becomes obvious that it is not from God when subjected to evaluation. To such individuals, those who lie in matters regarding God, are given a grave warning:

And who is more unjust than one who invents a lie about Allah or says, "It has been inspired to me," while nothing has been inspired to him, and one who says, "I will reveal [something] like what Allah revealed." And if you could but see when the wrongdoers are in the overwhelming pangs of death while the angels extend their hands, [saying], "Discharge your souls! Today you will be awarded the punishment of [extreme] humiliation for what you used to say against Allah other than the truth and [that] you were, toward His verses, being arrogant." [6: 93][1].

Dismissing Muhammad (may Allah bless him and grant him peace) as a Prophet, thus eliminating the Quran as a revelation.

Many Prophets who were sent had clear miracles given to them from God, such as Moses with his stick and Jesus reviving the dead (may Allah grant them peace). On the other hand, Muhammad (may Allah bless him and grant him peace) had no easily detectable miracles, and many people used that as an excuse to disbelieve in him. They argued that if he had a miracle or an indisputable sign they would've believed in him, but God condemns them questioningly:

And they say, "'Why does he not bring us a sign from his Lord?" Has there not come to them evidence of what was in the former scriptures? [133] And if We had destroyed them with a punishment before him, they would have said, "Our Lord, why did You not send to us a messenger so we could have followed Your verses before we were humiliated and disgraced?" [20: 133–134][1].

So, in addition to the fact that he had all the features of the awaited Prophet that they were foretold about in their scriptures, he also had miracles. These miracles though weren't as easily discernible as other Prophets' miracles, and when they discerned them they didn't want to acknowledge them as miracles.

The biggest miracle of which is the Quran that was revealed to him, for it foretold of some worldly events yet to happen. Such an event was the coming victory of the Romans over their assailants within just a few years. This at a time when they had just been defeated. Moreover, the Quran contained scientific facts that are being discovered till this day (detailed in section: Raw facts for Scientists).

Also, the fact that he could recite to people such elegant verses, progressive upon previous scriptures, although he was illiterate (couldn't read or write) is a miracle in itself. All this but alas, they refused but to be obstinate.

Moreover, their asking for a miracle or undisputable sign to believe in him, after rejecting the signs in the Quran, is not a sincere request since they will not abide by it. This was especially evident with the atheists and polytheists who requested a sign from him, whom God reproached saying:

And if not that a disaster should strike them for what their hands put forth [of sins] and they would say, "Our Lord, why did You not send us a messenger so we could have followed Your verses and been among the believers?"... [47] But when the truth came to them from Us, they said, "Why was he not given like that which was given to Moses?" Did they not disbelieve in that which was given to Moses before? They said, "[They are but] two works of magic supporting each other, and indeed we are, in both, disbelievers." [48] Say, "Then bring a scripture from Allah which is more guiding than either of them that I may follow it, if you should be truthful." [49] But if they do not respond to you - then know that they only follow their [own] desires. And who is more astray than one who follows his desire without guidance from Allah? Indeed, Allah does not guide the wrongdoing people. [50] And We have [repeatedly] conveyed to them the Qur'an that they might be reminded. [20: 47–51][1].

This is the core dilemma, that many people did see the incredible miracles of Moses (supported by his brother) and Jesus (peace be upon them) and yet disbelieved in them. Some people went even further and attempted to kill the Prophets. This ruled out that an incredible visible miracle is a definite factor which will make them believe.

In spite of all these points, God indeed did send a single, non-recurring but conclusive miracle to Muhammad (may Allah bless him and grant him peace). This was because the pagan Arabs stressed to the Messenger that they needed a sign, so he asked God for one hoping they will believe him, and God sent it to eliminate any excuse for not believing. The incredible miracle and clear sign was that God split the moon, yet this was the response of the pagans when it happened:

The Hour has come near, and the moon has split [in two]. [1] And if they see a miracle, they turn away and say, "Passing magic." [2] And they denied and followed their inclinations. But for every matter is a [time of] settlement. [3] And there has already come to them of information that in which there is deterrence - [4] Extensive wisdom - but warning does not avail [them]. [54: 1–5][1].

On the other hand, some people did acknowledge such miracles, but resorted to undermining his integrity through various accusations. The concept they wished to propagate is that he had contradictions or flaws that deem his message suspicious, on grounds that he is unfit or untrustworthy to be a carrier of God's message in the first place. This way, they could justify rejecting the Quran, and that is their ulterior motive.

Prophet Muhammad (may Allah bless him and grant him peace) was accused of lying, being crazy, being a magician, being a poet, and being a fortune-teller; all to discredit him in some way. But all of those accusations were logically annulled by God in the Quran. For example, concerning the accusation that the Prophet compiled the Quran himself (invented it, or assembled it from previous scriptures) and then lied that it was from God, God presented a fair challenge. This was to segregate those who were truly objective and wanted to reach the truth from the biased:

'Or, do they say: He has forged it. Say: Then bring ten forged chapters like it and call upon whom you can besides Allah, if you are truthful [13] But if they do not answer you, then know that it is revealed by Allah's knowledge and that there is no God but He; will you then submit (become Muslims)?' [11: 13–14][6]. God made this challenge simpler later in Muhammad's life (may Allah bless him and grant him peace), because the doubters were incapable of doing this, and just one chapter (sura)

was requested. *'Or do they say [about the Prophet], "He invented it?" Say, "Then bring forth a surah like it and call upon [for assistance] whomever you can besides Allah, if you should be truthful."* [10: 38][1].

Even before the start of the revelation of the Quran to Muhammad (may Allah bless him and grant him peace), he had lived amongst his tribe for 40 years. So they knew him well, and everyone would testify about his great manners and fine morals, and they were certain that he never lied before. They also knew that he was illiterate, yet he suddenly began reciting such eloquent verses, which indicated that it couldn't be from himself.

But when they disclosed that what he is reciting is bothering them, and that he should exchange or modify it (till it approves of their immoral habits and discriminative lifestyle), it carried the insinuation that he is lying. Modifying the Quran would mean that he is self-compiling the verses and that it isn't from God. So instead of being grateful that they were blessed with a revelation from God delivered to them by a Messenger from amidst them, they were placing terms to accept it. Consequently, God ordered him to inform them:

Say, "If Allah had willed, I would not have recited it to you, nor would He have made it known to you, for I had remained among you a lifetime before it. Then will you not reason?" [16] *So who is more unjust than he who invents a lie about Allah or denies His signs? Indeed, the criminals will not succeed* [10: 16–17][1].

Important to note is that his illiteracy was intended by God to avoid inciting their doubtfulness. If he could read, they would have the justification to suspect that he read the old scriptures thus learned what was in them, and ultimately self-compiling the Quran. Hence, the accusation that he made up the Quran is actually groundless, and yet ironically some people still claim so till today. *'Neither did you (O Muhammad SAW) read any book before it (this Quran), nor did you write any book (whatsoever) with your right hand. In that case, indeed, the followers of falsehood might have doubted'* [29: 48][2].

But even this accusation was refuted logically in the Quran, as some people may truly believe that he learned it from previous scholars of Judaism and Christianity instead of reading the scriptures. Allah said *'And indeed We know that they (polytheists and pagans) say: "It is only a human being who teaches him (Muhammad SAW)." The tongue of the man they refer to is foreign, while this (the Quran) is a clear Arabic tongue.'* [16: 103][2]. This is a crucial point, that the scriptures and scholars they accuse him of learning the verses from are originally foreign in language (not Arabic), yet the Quran is powerful in Arabic.

Moreover, the Quran informs the Jews and Christians about some points that they themselves did not know, such as the miracle that Jesus (peace be upon him) could speak when he was new-born. Thus how could the Quran be a copy or modification of previous Scriptures when it adds facts to the previous Scriptures? They are facts that weren't mentioned in previous Scriptures or have been lost through the centuries, yet were known amongst the people who met Prophets Moses and Jesus (peace be upon them).

One peculiar point that proves that Muhammad (may Allah bless him and grant him peace) did not make up the Quran himself is that it contains verses that go against him. For example, there are verses that threaten him if he does not deliver all of what God sent to him, or if he alters some verses, such as this one:

And indeed, they were about to tempt you away from that which We revealed to you in order to [make] you invent about Us something else; and then they would have taken you as a friend. [73] And if We had not strengthened you, you would have almost inclined to them a little. [74] Then [if you had], We would have made you taste double [punishment in] life and double [after] death. Then you would not find for yourself against Us a helper. [17: 73–75][1].

Other verses pointed out an error he made in judgement (but he did not sin, there is a difference), and reproached him gently about it. This was due to him frowning in the face of a blind man who came to ask him about Islam, and then deserted this man because he was busy talking to a person with status about Islam.

The Prophet frowned and turned away [1] Because there came to him the blind man, [interrupting]. [2] But what would make you perceive, [O Muhammad], that perhaps he might be purified [3] Or be reminded and the remembrance would benefit him? [4] As for he who thinks himself without need, [5] To him you give attention. [6] And not upon you [is any blame] if he will not be purified. [7] But as for he who came to you striving [for knowledge] [8] While he fears [Allah], [9] From him you are distracted. [80: 1–10][1].

There is also a verse which publicized a personal secret of his, and ordered him to violate his desire. It spoke of an incident in which God had revealed to him that a child he sponsored as a son (named Zayd) will eventually want to divorce his wife, and that the Prophet should marry her. God decreed this to abolish a bad custom amongst the pagan Arabs, which is that they considered a sponsored orphan to be the same as a biological son.

Upon that custom, it was unacceptable for a sponsor to marry the divorcee of whom he is sponsoring. Thus God ordered the Prophet (may Allah bless him and grant him peace) to establish a rule, by this procedure, that sponsored orphans should not be cut-off from their true lineage and then adjoined to the sponsor's lineage. This resulted in the forbidding of matters such as bestowing the orphan with the sponsors surname instead of his real father's surname, taking from the orphan's inheritance, etc.

However, when the time came and Zayd admitted to him that he wanted to divorce his wife, the Prophet told him to keep holding on to her. He did this to avoid clashing with the customs of the Arabs, especially considering that he didn't want to stir conflicts that may drive people away from accepting Islam.

But there is no compromise regarding God's will and laws, nor is it permissible for anyone to place his desires over God's will, even a Messenger. So in this upcoming verse, God exposed the Prophet's intentions, and ordered him to carry out what He decreed.

And [remember, O Muhammad], when you said to the one on whom Allah bestowed favor and you bestowed favor, "Keep your wife and fear Allah," while you concealed within yourself that which Allah is to disclose. And you feared the people, while Allah has more right that you fear Him. So when Zayd had no longer any need for her, We married her to you in order that there not be upon the believers any discomfort concerning the wives of their adopted sons when they no longer have need of them. And ever is the command of Allah accomplished. [33: 37][1].

The core point from the incidents that were just mentioned is: if a person compiles a book to attract followers and fame, why would he leave in verses that deduct from his greatness and glory in the eyes of people? Such verses emphasize that he can be punished too, that he makes judgemental errors (though scarcely), and that he is just a slave to God, receiving orders from Him which he must fulfil.

Returning to the topic about the accusations, he couldn't be a madman either since what he recited was too structured and sensible to come from a mentally handicapped person. Nor was he a poet, since the content and complexity of the verses surpassed human inspiration, as testified to by elite poets. Neither was he a magician because, ironically, some of the disbelievers themselves testified that he couldn't perform miracles. He wasn't a fortune teller either, since his behaviour was not of someone who knew what the future held except of which God had revealed to him, otherwise he would have avoided any harm from afflicting him:

Say, "I hold not for myself [the power of] benefit or harm, except what Allah has willed. And if I knew the unseen, I could have acquired much wealth, and no harm would have touched me. I am not except a warner and a bringer of good tidings to a people who believe." [7: 188][1].

One of the more absurd allegations is that the devils inspired him with the verses which make up the Quran. This was obviously refuted by God with a very simple concept, that what the Quran preaches is not pleasing for the devils *'It would neither suit them nor would they be able (to produce it)'* [45: 21–22][2]. So how could they have created it, or why even merely deliver it to a messenger, when it goes against their intentions and plans?

The Quran orders Muslims to worship God alone, to take the devil as an enemy, to be fair with people, treat the parents honourably, preserve family bonds, help the needy regularly, be good to neighbours and such. This while the devil wants to spread corruption and make mankind commit evil, so how can he be part of delivering a message that orders goodwill and forbids evil?

Generally, all these accusations were negated by God in that every messenger was met with the same set of accusations. This set of accusations was so identically recurring throughout generations to the extent that it may seem transmitted. It was as if the generations of disbelievers have met and advised each other of what to say about their Prophets, in order to justify disbelieving in them.

God censures such slanderers of Muhammad (may Allah bless him and grant him peace), and informs us about them with a peculiar description. He said *'Likewise, no Messenger came to those before them, but they said: "A sorcerer or a madman!" [52] Have they (the people of the past) transmitted this saying to these (Quraish pagans)? Nay, they are themselves a people transgressing beyond bounds (in disbelief)!'* [51: 52–53][2].

So God censures those disbelievers in that they are saying exactly what the disbelievers from generations before them said, and yet they imagine they came up with a unique argument. Every Prophet was met with arrogant disbelievers who wanted to harm him, and others who attempt to murder him. This fact is pointed out by God, together with the fact that Muhammad's coming was foretold by Jesus as "Ahmad", which is a synonym to Muhammad in the Arabic language (may Allah bless them and grant them peace). The Quranic verses state:

And [mention, O Muhammad], when Moses said to his people, "O my people, why do you harm me while you certainly know that I am the messenger of Allah to you?" And when they deviated, Allah caused their hearts to deviate. And Allah does not guide the defiantly disobedient people. [5] And [mention] when Jesus, the son of Mary, said, "O children of Israel, indeed I am the messenger of Allah to you confirming what came before me of the Torah and bringing good tidings of a messenger to come after me, whose name is Ahmad." But when he came to them with clear evidences, they said, "This is obvious magic." [61: 5–6][1].

Another method they resorted to, in order to reject the Quran, was denying that Muhammad (may Allah bless him and grant him peace) was the awaited Messenger, and that they will await the true one. That was because if they admitted he was the Messenger, and hence that the Quran is the book of God, they will have to change their lifestyles and won't be special anymore (since their holy books would become obsolete). So they denied he is the awaited Messenger although he carried all the signs of identifying him that were stated in the Scriptures. But God confronts them about this attitude:

O people of the Scripture! (Jews and Christians): "Why do you disbelieve in the Ayat of Allah, [the Verses about Prophet Muhammad SAW present in the Taurat (Torah) and the Injeel (Gospel)] while you (yourselves) bear witness (to their truth)." [70] O people of the Scripture (Jews and Christians): "Why do you mix truth with falsehood and conceal the truth while you know?" [3: 70–71][2].

This act is practically a war on God's will, since they commit a lot of corruption just to deny that Muhammad (may Allah bless him and grant him peace) is a true Messenger. Moreover, they tempt those who believe and follow the Messenger towards immorality and bodily pleasures, in order to lead them astray and make his message perish by fading. They are, in actuality, trying to eradicate God's word:

Say, "O Population of the Book, (Or: Family of the Book, i.e., the Jews and Christians) why do you bar from the way of Allah him who has believed (while you) inequitably seek to make it crooked, and you are witnesses?" And in no way is Allah ever heedless of whatever you do. [3: 99][3].

Nonetheless, to further confront them that he is their awaited Messenger, God points out to them that many of the scholars of the previous Scriptures identified Muhammad (may Allah bless him and grant him peace) and followed him into Islam. God says '*And indeed, it is [mentioned] in the scriptures of former peoples. [196] And has it not been a sign to them that it is recognized by the scholars of the Children of Israel?*' [26: 196–197][1] (Israel was a grandson of Ibrahim, Jacob to be precise, may Allah grant them peace).

This embarrassed them and made it evident without a doubt that they are just being arrogant. This was the case because not only did they find the identifying signs in Muhammad (may Allah bless him and grant him peace), but moreover that there were knowledgeable scholars amongst them who bore witness that he is the awaited Messenger.

God enlightens us on their motives for denying it, while scolding them logically. It comes '*Say: "See ye? If (this teaching) be from Allah, and ye reject it, and a witness from among the Children of Israel testifies to its similarity (with earlier scripture), and has believed while ye are arrogant, (how unjust ye are!) truly, Allah guides not a people unjust."* [46: 10][5].

Another ground upon which Jews and Christians rejected the authenticity of Muhammad (may Allah bless him and grant him peace), and hence Islam, was that they are special to God. An array of faulty reasoning led them to this assumption, such as that a Prophet cannot be sent from God from outside their lineage (regarding Jews: that of Isaac's, peace be upon him), that salvation cannot be through anyone other than Jesus (peace be upon him), or that they are the older and original religions, which makes them better and more righteous.

So the people of former Scriptures faced the Muslims and told them that being Jews/Christians is better for them than being Muslims, on grounds that they will be more guided to the righteous path. However, God instructed Muhammad to bring them to terms with this reality:

Say, [O Muhammad], "Do you argue with us about Allah while He is our Lord and your Lord? For us are our deeds, and for you are your deeds. And we are sincere [in deed and intention] to Him." [139] Or do you say that Abraham and Ishmael and Isaac and Jacob and the Descendants were Jews or Christians? Say, "Are you more knowing or is Allah?" And who is more unjust than one who conceals a testimony he has from Allah? And Allah is not unaware of what you do. [2: 139–140][1].

This argument faces them with a multitude of logical points. One of them is that God is the Lord of all the people, which they cannot deny, hence being special/supreme is not exclusive to their lineage, otherwise it would be an injustice done from God. God is highly exalted above doing an injustice; injustice is a consequence of humans being a flawed creature.

Another point is that if they look at their actions and that of Muslims in general, they will find that they commit more sins even according to their own books. Thus, how can they be more special to God when they disobey God more? Also, how can they be more special to God when Muslims are sincere and direct all their worship to God alone, whereas other factions distribute their worship between God and others (e.g. Jesus, Holy Spirit, angels, idols)?

Moreover, how can it be said that one cannot enter heaven except if he is a Jew/Christian when a core belief of theirs is that they follow the Prophet Ibrahim (peace be upon him), who was neither a Jew nor

Christian? Then, God reprimands those who withheld their testimony that Muhammad (may Allah bless him and grant him peace) expressed the signs they were foretold about regarding the awaited prophet, and for concealing that Ibrahim (peace be upon him) was neither Jew nor Christian.

Concluding this topic, it needs to be pointed out that Muhammad (may Allah bless him and grant him peace) is one of the most misconceived characters by non-Muslims. This is due to the intentional tarnishing done by a segment of non-Muslims, which then spreads by hearsay and is believed by the public. Many of the non-Muslims who repeat defamatory statements about Prophet Muhammad do not realize how concerned he is about the well-being of humanity, or how important, righteous and beneficial he is even to those who don't believe in him. Prophet Muhammad instructs his followers to be good to people in general, setting a basic guide on how we should treat others by saying:

He who desires to be shifted from the fire of Hell and to enter Heaven, death should come to him while he is in a state of belief in Allah and the Last Day, and should do unto others what he loves to be done unto him.[8]

The last statement means that we should not to do anything unto anyone which we would not like to be done to us. In other words, we should treat people how we would like people to treat us, and this good is reflected even upon those who don't believe in Muhammad. But even if we set this point aside, many non-Muslims don't know that Prophet Muhammad (may Allah grant him peace and blessings) will stand up for them on Judgement day in certain issues, despite that they don't acknowledge him and may even have attacked him! Prophet Muhammad warned us Muslims:

If anyone wrongs a [non-Muslim] man with whom a covenant has been made, or curtails any right of his, or imposes on him more

than he can bear, or takes anything from him without his ready agreement, I shall be his adversary on the day of resurrection.[2]

So I am forewarned that if I do injustice to a non-Muslim whom is peaceful, Prophet Muhammad -whom I follow- will argue, in front of God, for the non-Muslim against me until that person's rights have been returned to him from me. That is who Muhammad is.

A rationale: if this was a message from God, He would have sent an Angel as His messenger, and not a human.

Firstly, we should comprehend that God does what He wills. It is an overstepping of boundaries for a person to say: God should have done this or that; for a human does not encompass all the knowledge or wisdom in the Universe to speculate over the decisions of who is All-Knowing and All-Wise.

After comprehending that, we can then discuss this matter at hand according to what God revealed to us. '*And what prevented the people from believing when guidance came to them except that they said, "Has Allah sent a human messenger?" [94] Say, "If there were upon the earth angels walking securely, We would have sent down to them from the heaven an angel [as a] messenger." [17: 94–95]*[1].

And this is a very logical rationale, since it is human nature to examine everything that is different from him. For example, when people see a strange creature, they gather around it and speculate about it. As a matter of fact, there have previously been media claims that some aliens have crashed on Earth, and that top government organizations have them under custody and are performing experiments on them. And although this is all alleged, it demonstrates the human behaviour, in that different species cannot be left alone to walk casually among humans. They will not be left freely.

Upon this excuse, some people rejected the Quran merely because the messenger was human and not an Angel. If only they had assessed the contents of the message objectively, but alas, their attention was focused at preserving their culture and lifestyle.

However, God knows that even if He sent them an angel, they would find another excuse to disbelieve. *'They swear their strongest oaths by Allah, that if a (special) sign came to them, by it they would believe. Say: "Certainly (all) signs are in the power of Allah: but what will make you (Muslims) realise that (even) if (special) signs came, they will not believe?"* [6: 109][2].

How can we not believe this fact when it is even historically documented that it did happen, for we know that Moses (may Allah grant him peace) had miracles and yet a faction of people did not believe him. Jesus (may Allah grant him peace) too had incredible miracles, but a faction still did not believe him. Yet on the other hand, when Muhammad (may Allah bless him and grant him peace) was sent but with no recurrently performable miracles, a faction of people discredited him on that account.

This happened in spite of the fact that some of them believe in previous Prophets who also couldn't perform miracles, such as Noah and Joseph (peace be upon them all). So the issue really doesn't revolve around the matter of performable miracles, since there will still be disbelievers whether a Prophet performs miracles or not. Those who do not want to accept the truth will discredit a Prophet one way or another.

Some even criticized the fact that he was a plain human, who used to eat and go to the market, to which God provided a reasoning for: *'And We did not send before you, [O Muhammad], any of the messengers except that they ate food and walked in the markets. And We have made some of you [people] as trial for others - will you have patience? And ever is your Lord, Seeing.'* [25: 20][1]. They did not bear in mind that the Prophets before him also ate food and went to markets, but that did not negate them from being Prophets. The Prophets truly were just humans after all, with human needs.

Neither did the disbelievers bear in mind that the Prophets are a test for people: will they believe them or not. Similarly, people are a test for the Prophets: will the Prophets be patient and continue calling people to the truth after the disbelievers fight them or not. Hence there is this part in the verse "And We have made some of you [people] as trial for others - will you have patience?".

If a Prophet fulfils everyone's desires, then everyone would believe in God and testing us on Earth would be pointless. The issue that God wills to test people about is whether they will believe in Him under His terms, not ours.

On a related topic, we now know that some disbelievers rejected the message from God because it was delivered by a human who is just like them, who eats, drinks, excretes, sleeps, and goes to the market. *'And they say, "What is this messenger that eats food and walks in the markets? Why was there not sent down to him an angel so he would be with him a warner?"* [25: 7][1]. Isn't it ironic that while they reject his message on accounts that he eats and so on, there are others who called Jesus (may Allah grant him peace) a God and worship him although he also eats and so on? How are there such extreme deviations in belief?

It is very likely that God, out of his ultimate knowledge and wisdom, did not bestow any recurrently performable miracles upon Muhammad lest the tragedy that arose from some of the followers of Jesus might reoccur from some followers of Muhammad (peace be upon them). The tragedy is considering him a God instead of a Prophet. If God sends a Messenger with astonishing miracles, he is worshiped; but if a Messenger without performable miracles is sent, he is discredited?

A rationale: If the Quran was the word of God, anyone who has read it would have believed in it.

This rationale is flawed, because some people stubbornly deny the truth using various methods even though they know it's the truth. They do so by lying, misinterpreting verses, or derogating from the Prophet's integrity. The reason for all this is to fulfil their own objectives, mainly to remain free to do whatever they desire in life.

They resort to such methods because accepting the truth would hinder fulfilling their desires, by putting boundaries on what they are allowed to do through 'right' and 'wrong'. In some instances, even religious figures practice this, by twisting meanings in holy verses to fit their motives, like rabbi, priests and sheikhs. The motive behind their treachery is to reach fame, fortune, or gain acknowledgement and contentment from a person with authority. And God informs us about this practice, telling us:

Do you covet [the hope, O believers], that they would believe for you while a party of them used to hear the words of Allah and then distort the Torah after they had understood it while they were knowing? [75] And when they meet those who believe, they say, "We have believed"; but when they are alone with one another they say "Do you talk to them about what Allah has revealed to you so they can argue with you about it before your Lord?" Then will you not reason? [76] But do they not know that Allah knows what they conceal and what they declare? [2: 75–77][1]. But God scolds them by questioning them:

Do they not ponder over the Word (of Allah), or has anything (new) come to them that did not come to their fathers of old? [68] Or do they not recognize their Messenger, that they deny him? [69] Or do they say, "He is possessed"? Nay, he has brought them the Truth, but most of them hate the Truth. [70] If the Truth had been in accord with their desires, truly the heavens and the earth, and all beings therein would have been in confusion and corruption! Nay, We have sent them their admonition, but they turn away from their admonition. [71] Or is it that thou askest them for some recompense? But the recompense of thy Lord is best: He is the Best of those who give sustenance. [72] But verily thou callest them to the Straight Way; [23: 68–73][2].

Truly, God had sent them the truth, but most of them hate the truth, and this is the harsh reality. All individuals know that stealing is wrong, yet this does not prevent some people from stealing. Even some very rich businessmen practice this under some excuse, which shows that not all people will follow the truth.

God describes Himself

Though the coming verse does not contain a logical argument and is mainly an informative one, however I felt I had to mention it. It is one of the greatest and most unique verses in the Quran, for in it, God speaks about Himself. All I request from the reader is to evaluate whether such a verse can be man-made, or does it way exceed a human's capacity. God says:

Allah - there is no deity except Him, the Ever-Living, the Sustainer of [all] existence. Neither drowsiness overtakes Him nor sleep. To Him belongs whatever is in the heavens and whatever is on the earth. Who is it that can intercede with Him except by His permission? He knows what is [presently] before them and what will be after them, and they encompass not a thing of His knowledge except for what He wills. His Kursi [throne] extends over the heavens and the earth, and their preservation tires Him not. And He is the Most High, the Most Great. [2: 255][1].

2.2 Accusations directed at Islam

An easy way of dismissing Islam as a viable religion, in an attempt to alleviate one's conscience, is to accuse it of being unjust or impractical. This way, the claimer can propagate that it should not, or cannot, be accepted and adopted. Answering all the accusations is beyond the scope of this book, so only a few accusations will be refuted. This is to set general basic concepts on how to evaluate Islam, and to encompass the schemes through which accusations are built. I cannot stress enough how important it is, for the seeker of truth, to read the Quran personally.

Women are treated unjustly in Islam?

Alas, the problem lies within Muslims who misunderstand or ignore the teachings of Islam, which in turn leads to violations against the rights of a woman. But a simple statement needs to be made: would a religion that belittles and oppresses women contain, in its Holy book, a guide for men about treating their wives, and a grave warning about defying these rules?

O you who have believed, it is not lawful for you to inherit women by compulsion, and do not make difficulties for them in order to take [back] part of what you gave them unless they commit a clear immorality. And live with them in kindness. For if you dislike them - perhaps you dislike a thing and Allah makes therein much good [19] But if you want to replace one wife with another and you have given one of them a great amount [in gifts], do not take [back] from it anything. Would you take it in injustice and manifest sin? [20] And how could you take it while you have gone in unto each other and they have taken from you a solemn covenant? [4: 19–21][1].

As we can see, even during a divorce men are given clear instructions with prohibitions on what isn't ethical to do, with a strong reprimand and threat to those who break them. This is just one example of how Islam advises men about treating women and respecting their rights. However, prejudiced individuals would rather focus on the woman's obligations such as covering her hair; laws that are set in order to protect the women themselves. Certainly, the one who created us is the most knowledgeable of what benefits us when setting laws.

Accusers intentionally avoid mentioning the rights that Islam bestows and protects a woman with (as in the mentioned verse), or the guides given to men about treating women. They do so in order to make their point of view look substantiated; to reach their goal of tarnishing Islam and subsequently, making people disregard it.

Accusations that women are considered inferior, or that they are just objects of pleasure, are clearly contradicted by some scripts in Islam. No matter what perspective the accusers present regarding this topic, it doesn't stand since this is what Prophet Muhammad (may Allah bless him and grant him peace) advised us with when a person asked him "Who among people is most deserving of my fine treatment?": he said "**Your mother**"; he asked "Then who?", the Prophet replied "**Your mother**"; he asked again "Then who?", the Prophet said "**Your mother**"; he asked once more "Then who?", the Prophet said "**Then your father**"[10].

Another incident is when a follower came to Prophet Muhammad (may Allah bless him and grant him peace) and said "O Messenger of Allah, I want to go out and fight (in Jihad), and I have come to ask your advice", he said "**Do you have a mother?**", he replied "Yes", he then said "**Then stay with her, for Paradise is beneath her feet**".[11] The meaning is that Paradise cannot be reached without the contentment of the mother, so a Muslim has to do his best in obeying, serving and pleasing his mother (except in a request that violates God's laws, i.e. if she commands him to do something sinful then he must refuse it but with gentleness).

These documented incidents are what we Muslims are actually being taught, which annuls even an argument that Muslims are trying to appear as if they don't belittle women. The accusers don't mention such teachings.

Islam is a religion of violence?

Another malicious accusation directed at Islam is that it is a religion of barbarianism and violence. Again, would a religion that causes its followers to behave as such have this in its Holy book:

O you who believe! Enter not houses other than your own, until you have asked permission and greeted those in them, that is better for you, in order that you may remember [27] And if you find no one therein, still, enter not until permission has been given. And if you are asked to go back, go back, for it is purer for you, and Allah is All-Knower of what you do. [24: 27–28][2].

If we notice, even the subject of visiting at an inappropriate time for the host has been covered. This is to prevent any party from harbouring negative feelings to the other, and to avoid any embarrassment for either party, for it is God who set the rules, which avoids controversy between individuals. So how is a religion that teaches its followers such elite manners when visiting friends, family and acquaintances, be a religion of barbarianism? In another chapter, God condones certain evil human habits (which some people see natural or harmless) to indicate how evil they are:

O you who believe! Avoid much suspicions, indeed some suspicions are sins. And spy not, neither backbite one another. Would one of you like to eat the flesh of his dead brother? You would hate it (so hate backbiting). And fear Allah. Verily, Allah is the One Who accepts repentance, Most Merciful. [49: 12][2].

God advises us to avoid frequent suspicion about others, because it is human nature to lean towards the worst case scenario, upon which unfounded reactions may be taken and hence wronging others. Then, He denounces spying and backbiting between people, and symbolizes backbiting, which usually causes slandering of another person's reputation, with eating his dead brother's flesh.

This is because mentioning a person's flaws in his absence is actually biting off chunks from that person's reputation until he is defamed, since his esteem dissipates until people disrespect him. Doing so is similar to biting pieces of that person's flesh; one is spiritual and the other is physical. Moreover, it symbolizes how despicable it is since the backbiter attacks someone at a moment when that person is not able to defend himself.

Returning to the issue about violence, Islam instructs its followers to lean towards peace with nations and avoid wishing for wars *'And if they incline to peace, then incline to it [also] and rely upon Allah. Indeed, it is He who is the Hearing, the Knowing.'* [8: 61][1]. The direction in Islam is that violence is permissible, sometimes even obligatory, in defending oneself when being assaulted or to establish justice. Islam is a religion that calls for peace, but it is not a pacifist religion that calls for passiveness with injustice.

But when force is permissible, it orders us to be fair even during retribution against an assaulting nation. God instructs us *'And do not let the hatred of a people for having obstructed you from al-Masjid al-Haram lead you to transgress. And cooperate in righteousness and piety, but do not cooperate in sin and aggression. And fear Allah; indeed, Allah is severe in penalty.'* [5: 2][1].

This principle is re-emphasized in a closely following verse *'O you who have believed, be persistently standing firm for Allah, witnesses in justice, and do not let the hatred of a people prevent you from being just. Be just; that is nearer to righteousness. And fear Allah; indeed, Allah is Acquainted with what you do.'* [5: 8][1]. Upon such, Muslims who do not abide by these rules are at fault and earned punishment from God upon this violation. The flaw lies within them personally.

And answering this accusation from world reality, how many Islamic countries are currently invading other countries? On the other hand, how many non-Islamic countries are invading Islamic countries? In that, is the answer to the accusation.

Islam is a religion that gives individuals the right to defend themselves, moreover, encourages it. If this right was abolished, then the world would live in darkness because evil would overtake justice, e.g. God's places of worship would be destroyed by the wicked and immoral people. More importantly, levels of humanitarian crimes and suffering would skyrocket, since the criminals will find only a few who forcefully stand up to them. God says:

To those against whom war is made, permission is given (to fight), because they are wronged;- and verily, Allah is most powerful for their aid;- [39] (They are) those who have been expelled from their homes in defiance of right,- (for no cause) except that they say, "our Lord is Allah". Did not Allah check one set of people by means of another, there would surely have been pulled down monasteries, churches, synagogues, and mosques, in which the name of Allah is commemorated in abundant measure. Allah will certainly aid those who aid his (cause);- for verily Allah is full of Strength, Exalted in Might, (able to enforce His Will). [22: 39–40][5].

Why are there 'beneficial' things that are forbidden?

The reality is that this line of thought is a false perception, resulting from lack of knowledge combined with some misunderstanding. For example, some people say that freedom of intercourse is a good thing for man, so why is a human's freedom tied up by making intercourse outside of marriage forbidden? The key answer is that this person sees only part of the big picture. He sees the benefit, the mood elevation, and not the detriments such as the destruction of social bonds on the long run, the loss of lineage tracking, unwanted pregnancies, abortions, spread of diseases, psychologically traumatized children and so on.

And the fact is, everything that God forbids is for a strong reason, which is that it is overall harmful to a human's well-being. God clarifies this to us in an example of wine and gambling, which became more comprehensible to us after recent studies have proven that there are benefits in drinking wine in moderation. These studies definitely encouraged some people to make drinking a habit. The problem is that such pleasures start controlled, but by time, as the body gets used to them (a phenomenon called tolerance), the individual needs to increase the dose and intensity to reach the same level of satisfaction or pleasure. This usually ends up with addiction.

The Quran which was sent down to us more than 1400 years ago, long before these studies about wine were carried out, contained this verse:

They ask you about wine and gambling; Say "In them is great sin and [yet, some] benefit for people, but their sin is greater than their benefit." And they ask you what they should spend; Say, "The excess [beyond needs]." Thus Allah makes clear to you the verses [of revelation] that you might give thought. [2: 219][1].

In the verse, wine and gambling, which are overall harmful to a person, were put into contrast with something beneficial instead, which is using the money for charity to help the needy. This accentuates the great difference in usefulness between both. So this is the basis behind forbidding such matters, since God is All-Knowing about every aspect of every matter, that their drawbacks outweigh their benefits. God gave us those examples to contemplate upon them.

2.3 Raw facts for scientists in the Quran

Before we talk about the facts, we should keep in mind that this Quran was revealed more than 1400 years ago and has never been altered. Thus, when we find different scientific facts in the Quran periodically being proven through experimentation, it is a recurring miracle. Moreover, it indicates that this book is not within the scope of a human's knowledge to compile.

When scientific facts in the Quran are verified, it eliminates any doubt about its authenticity (that it is from God) under any pretence, especially after failing to find a single scientific fact in the Quran that is wrong. Moreover, there are scientific facts in the Quran that are still to be discovered and proven scientifically by future generations with technological advancements.

For example, it is stated that eleven planets are orbiting the Sun, which will be verified in the future possibly with the development of stronger telescopes. When such a fact is verified, it has the effect of repeatedly demonstrating to generation after generation that the book, Quran, is a miracle. Prophet Joseph (may Allah grant him peace) saw this vision '*As Yusuf (Joseph) said to his father, "O my father, surely I saw (i.e., in a dream) eleven planets and the sun and the moon; I saw them prostrating to me."* [12: 4][3].

Elaborating on the topic about planets, currently after Pluto has been disregarded, it is said that eight planets are orbiting the Sun. But evidence of the presence of a new planet has appeared as of year

2016. When they find that planet, they will declare that there are 9 planets again, and this will keep recurring till they find the 11 planets. Briefly explained, very distant galactic bodies were found moving in an orbiting pattern around an obvious strong gravitational core point, definitely indicating the presence of a large planet, which they are searching for.

Generally, for those who would like to know about all the scientific facts mentioned in the Quran and in scientific detail, they should refer to specialized books. Venturing deeply into this subject is beyond the field of this book; however, here are a few examples:

Recently, it has been theorized and accepted that the whole universe was previously just a compact hot mass of very high density, which then inflated, giving rise to everything around us (sun, stars, planets, black holes, etc.). That is the Big Bang theory. Scientists say that the high density mass resulted in some sort of smoke, which is a fact that was conveyed to us over 1400 years ago *'Then He directed Himself to the heaven while it was smoke and said to it and to the earth "Come [into being], willingly or by compulsion." They said "We have come willingly."* [41: 11][1]. This smoke cooled down and condensed, forming galactic bodies such as stars and planets.

An interesting fact that is a basis in this theory is that the universe is still in expansion (possibly from the initial explosion), so one can rightfully say that we are living within an explosion that is still taking place! Yet, God made the conditions suitable and stable enough for us on Earth to survive. So not only the origin of the universe is stated in the Quran, but also that it is still expanding *'And the heaven We constructed with strength, and indeed, We are [its] expander'* [51: 47][1].

He created all that is around us for us to ponder upon His creation, and He organized them so that they would serve us. It comes in the Quran:

Do you not see that Allah has made subject to you whatever is in the heavens and whatever is in the earth and amply bestowed upon you

His favors, [both] apparent and unapparent? But of the people is he who disputes about Allah without knowledge or guidance or an enlightening Book [from Him]. [31: 20][1].

Returning to the topic of the Big Bang theory, it must be noted that it is relatively recent and based on scientific evidence. What's interesting is that it is in accordance with what God had already said about the origin of the universe:

Do not the Unbelievers see that the heavens and the earth were joined together (as one unit of creation), before we clove them asunder? We made from water every living thing. Will they not then believe? [30] And We have set on the earth mountains standing firm, lest it should shake with them, and We have made therein broad highways (between mountains) for them to pass through: that they may receive Guidance. [31] And We made the sky a protected ceiling, but they, from its signs, are turning away. [32] And it is He who created the night and the day and the sun and the moon; all [heavenly bodies] in an orbit are swimming. [21: 30–33][2].

So what does this conformity tell us? Furthermore, the following is for advanced scientists: on the events preceding judgment day, God informs us that the sky will split and the Earth will be shuddered and crumbled. Eventually, the skies and the Earth will be replaced with similar entities. God says '*[It will be] on the Day the earth will be replaced by another earth, and the heavens [as well], and all creatures will come out before Allah, the One, the Prevailing*' [14: 48][1]; ('heavens' here meaning the skies).

The proof of why and how this will happen is not definite yet, but in that field is scope for researching, and perhaps they will figure it out. Worthy of mention is what some scientists theorized regarding this topic. They suggested that when energy of the universe's expansion from the Big Bang explosion dissipates, the galaxy will start shrinking and reuniting till it forms the hot compact dense mass again, with a possible re-explosion.

And to list some other scientific facts that were present in the Quran before they were discovered or proven with research, there is the strange phenomenon that the water in the different seas does not mix although they meet. This is due to the difference in composition (as if a preventive barrier is between them) *'Is not He (Most Charitable) Who made the earth a residence, and made amidst it rivers, and made for it anchorages (i.e. firm mountains), and made a partition between the two seas? Is there a god with Allah? No indeed, (but) most of them do not know'* [27: 61][3].

Recently, via functional magnetic resonance imaging (fMRI), it has been noticed that the forebrain (prefrontal cortex) is the part of the brain responsible for fabricating lies that a person intends to say. That has been indicated to us over 1400 years ago in Quranic verses, in which God warns a certain disbeliever about lying to defy God's message *'Nay! if he desist not, We would certainly smite his forehead, [15] A lying, sinful forehead'* [96: 15–16][6].

It was also discovered that light does not reach deep underwater, which we were informed about together with the fact that the darkness occurs in layers. This is due to the fact that each colour in the light spectrum can penetrate the water to a different depth according to its wavelength, so each stops at a level/layer of water. This was revealed at a time when there was no diving equipment for people to reach such deep sea levels and know this information, and the verse is a similitude to the spiritual state of a disbeliever:

Or like utter darkness in the deep sea: there covers it a wave above which is another wave, above which is a cloud, (layers of) utter darkness one above another; when he holds out his hand, he is almost unable to see it; and to whomsoever Allah does not give light, he has no light. [24: 40][6].

God informed us about the development of man, from where we originated and then how new lives form, mentioning that we pass through phases while developing, within three darknesses. Scientists have later discovered that the embryo is indeed protected by three walls, each does not permit light (the abdominal wall, the uterine wall, and the amniotic sac with its fluid).

He created you from one soul. Then He made from it its mate, and He produced for you from the grazing livestock eight mates. He creates you in the wombs of your mothers, creation after creation, within three darknesses. That is Allah, your Lord; to Him belongs dominion. There is no deity except Him, so how are you averted? [39: 6][1].

At a certain phase, an embryos appearance in its mother's womb has been described as something chewed, and it wasn't until recently that magnification devices have displayed an embryo in the womb. The resulting images showed surprising resemblance to the Quranic description. How did the Quran contain information about the stages of development of a baby when it was revealed in a period where there was no radiographic, ultrasonic or magnetic imaging of any sort? The verse reads:

O you mankind, in case you are suspicious as to the Rising again, then surely We created you from dust, thereafter from a sperm-drop, thereafter from a clot, (i.e., embryo) thereafter from a chewed up morsel in shapely created form and other than shapely created (from) that We make (it) evident for you. And We make to reside in the wombs whatever We decide till a stated term, thereafter We bring you out as young children, (Literally: as a child) thereafter that you may reach full age. And among you there is he who is taken up, (i.e., dies) and among you there is he who is turned back to the most decrepit age, so that even after (some) knowledge, he knows nothing (Literally: he does not know a thing). And you see the earth torpid; then when We send down water upon it, it shakes and swells and grows of every (growth) a delightful pair. [22: 5][2].

Another interesting fact is that the main source of Iron for some ancient civilizations was from the Earth's crust, utilizing it in ornaments and weaponry. It was discovered that many meteorites bombarded Earth before mankind dwelled, supplying the Earth's crust with its large percent of Iron. The phrasing in the Quran indicated that Iron was sent down to Earth:

We have already sent Our messengers with clear evidences and sent down with them the Scripture and the balance that the people may maintain [their affairs] in justice. And We sent down iron, wherein is great military might and benefits for the people, and so that Allah may make evident those who support Him and His messengers unseen. Indeed, Allah is Powerful and Exalted in Might. [57: 25][1].

Another intriguing scientific fact is that the surface area of the Earth's land is diminishing. This fact was stated in the Quran, with a specific detail that it happens from its borders.

Say, "Who can protect you at night or by day from the Most Merciful?" But they are, from the remembrance of their Lord, turning away. [42] Or do they have gods to defend them other than Us? They are unable [even] to help themselves, nor can they be protected from Us. [43] But, [on the contrary], We have provided good things for these [disbelievers] and their fathers until life was prolonged for them. Then do they not see that We set upon the land, reducing it from its borders? So it is they who will overcome? [44] Say, "I only warn you by revelation." But the deaf do not hear the call when they are warned. [21: 42–45][1].

One method by which this occurs is due to ice glaciers melting and expanding seawater from global warming. This causes sea levels to rise and engulf seacoast land through time, almost unnoticeably (Figure 1).

Returning to the topic about the galaxy, explosions of galactic bodies look like 'roses' (Figure 2). Similarly, we are foretold that the sky will split open and look like a rose on judgement day, and that it will have 'doors' (in another verse). This flowery pattern denotes the disintegration of a galactic body, a supernova *'And when the heaven splitteth asunder and becometh rosy like red hide-'* [55: 37][4] ('heaven' here means the sky).

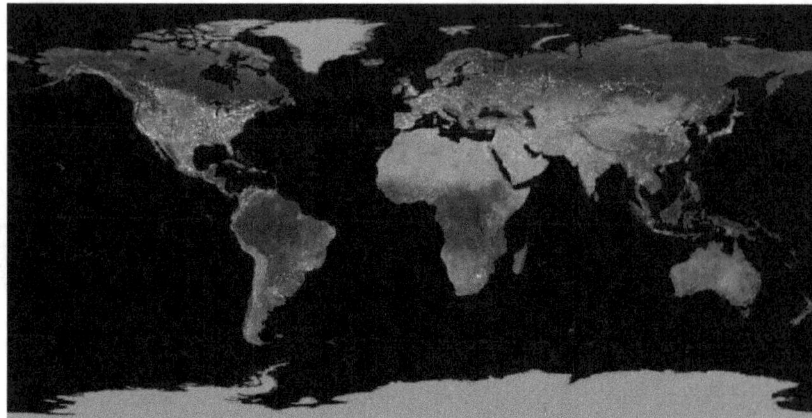

Figure 1: Red areas depict submerging coastlines over years due to rising sea levels from global warming (courtesy of NASA).

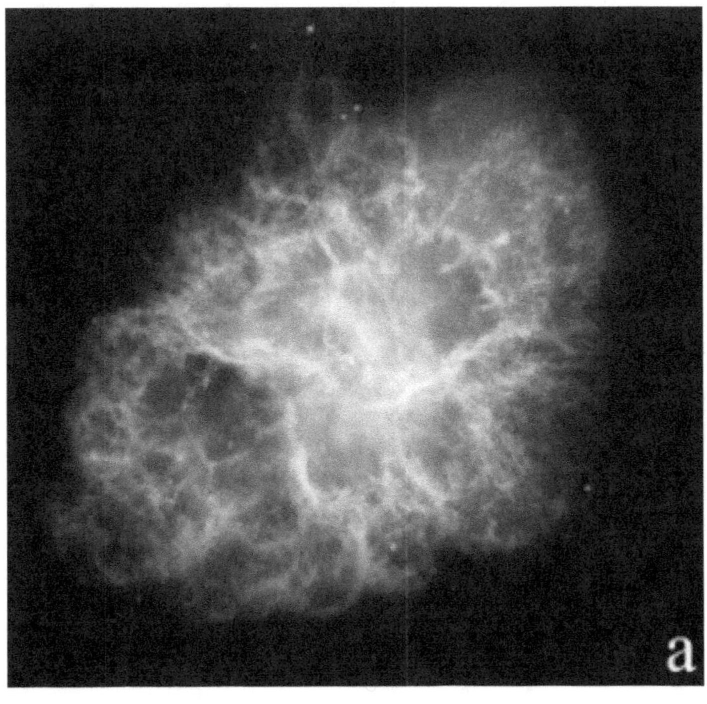

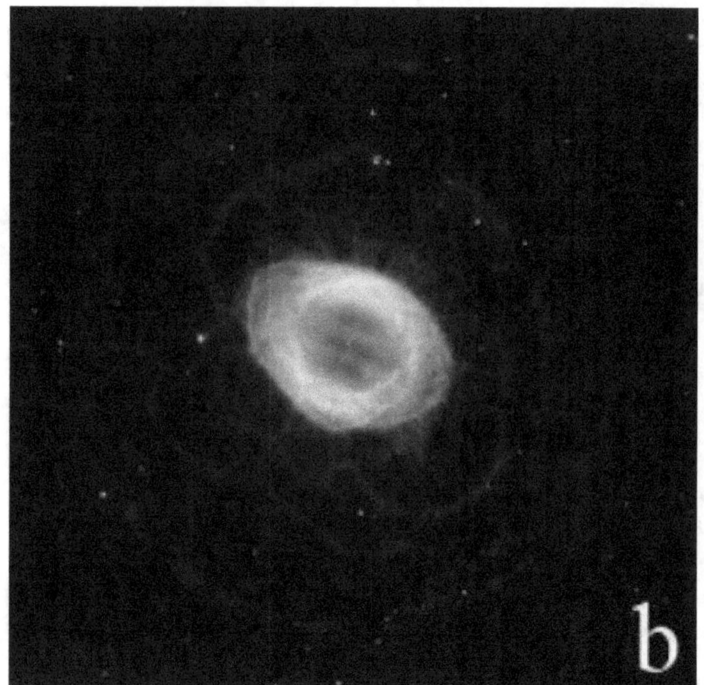
b

c

d

Figure 2a and 2b show supernovas (courtesy of NASA); while figure 2c and 2d show roses. Note the similarities in features.

What's worth noticing is that many verses usually don't discuss these facts specifically, rather, the verses talk about a general topic which includes a scientific phenomenon. Thus, these scientific facts are indicated within the context of the verses. This means that whoever created these verses has absolute knowledge about the structure of the creations (Earth and skies). Thus they cannot come from any human, or even an angel; they must be from a higher and divine source. This is supported by the fact that the verses surpass just mentioning definite scientific facts, but rather refer to them within a bigger context.

Lastly, I would like to ask every scientist a question: what keeps the laws of physics (and other laws) from deviating? In other words, why does any law of physics give the same outcome in 100% of the trials? Why don't these laws deviate even once? For example, when I throw a bouncing ball, why does it bounce back always and never once does it stick to the ground!? If anyone ponders long and hard upon this, he will reach the conclusion that there must be a God who prevents these laws from going astray.

Let us suppose that at a nuclear power station they split an atom to extract energy from it, yet no energy came out of it. Who are we going to complain to that can do something about what happened? And what are we going to complain about, that we got no energy from a splitting atom? Factually, that was a law we deduced upon observation of what naturally happens; we did not create that law, we just created a formula for it. So, if in one of a million instances nothing happens when we split an atom, what can we do?

What if a planet, which is balanced in orbit around the Sun by centrifugal force, suddenly deviates from its path and goes out of orbit, ignoring the centrifugal law, and goes about colliding with other planets? Who will we complain to that it broke a fundamental law?

Thus there must be a God who preserves the universe, monitoring the laws of physics from going astray even once, lest chaos would ensue.

Every aspect of the Universe has submitted to God's rules willingly, and the proof of their submission is the order evident in the Universe, leaving the humans and Jinn still divided between submitting willingly (by worship) or by compulsion (the rule of death, which no one has overcome). The Universe has been preserved for millions of years due to its unflawed obedience to God's laws. But it must have an appointed age, and there must be a point where it will stop, just as any energy source is deemed to run out.

The question then will be: who has submitted to God willingly in his life? '*So is it other than the religion of Allah they desire, while to Him have submitted [all] those within the heavens and earth, willingly or by compulsion, and to Him they will be returned?*' [3: 83][1].

So praise be to Allah, who bestowed upon us free will (the ability to disobey Him), but did not bestow such an ability to the laws of physics otherwise they would go haywire every once in a while. Imagine our lives if the laws of physics around us could stray like us, i.e. if they are as dependable as us humans!?

In conclusion to this chapter, it is clear that some non-Muslims aggressively attack Islam to show that their religion is the righteous religion, and it has been demonstrated how gravely wrong they are in their claims. Yet, this does not stop them from restating their claims. That is because a conflict of interest has occurred. For example, when a Jew talks about Islam, he will have to derogate from it to show that he is on the right path.

He does so because if he praises Islam, then it would be expected from him to become a Muslim to have integrity, since he admits that it is a more righteous religion. This integrity, by making what he does and what he says in accord with each other, gives him credibility with people. Likewise, when I talk about Christianity, it is obvious that I will point out its errors since I see that Islam is the rightful religion. It is a conflict of interest for me to praise Christianity.

So asking a non-Muslim about Islam creates a conflict of interest, and asking a Muslim about another religion does so too; it will be a biased opinion. Therefore, I advise the seeker for truth (the reader) to avoid placing people in a state of conflict of interest while seeking the truth. Thus, just as he heard from me the rebuttal to the accusations directed at Islam, he should ask (for example) a Jewish scholar about the flaws I mentioned regarding Judaism and hear his responses. Then, it is up to the seeker himself to assess and deduce what makes more sense and who is more righteous (hence truthful).

The bottom line is that there is a book that exists (Quran) which contains numerous truthful points, prophecies that have been fulfilled, and logical aspects in its verses. What are we supposed to do with such a book? Ignore or deny it? Struggle to conceal it? Why? To us Muslims, this book is so authentic to an extent that it authenticates what we cannot verify. It authenticates aspects which we cannot see or validate currently, such as the coming of judgement day, and the existence of Heaven and Hell. There simply isn't any possible reasonable explanation for this book except that it MUST be from God.

That is why we believe in it and everything it informs us about, such as that there is just one God, the Almighty. Furthermore, it informs us that the Prophets and Holy Books are a chain, and that judgement day will definitely befall. There is no need to blindly follow the Quran, it presents verifications regarding itself for those who wish to check its authenticity.

After demonstrating that Islam is a valid and rightful religion on a personal level, the next methical question comes naturally, and is a critical one. The question is: if Islam is an attested religion, as was Judaism and Christianity, what are the parameters by which a person should choose his religion? This is the subject of the next chapter.

Chapter 3: Which religion should a person follow?

Following the discussion of faulty aspects in popular beliefs and that Islam is a valid religion, the next logical step is to decide which of those beliefs (or religions) is the most eligible to follow. Here we will discuss how to free a person initially by allowing free-thought, through disengaging him from a binding concept that although is instinctive, but can be of devastating consequences. This instinctive concept is that a person must adopt the religion or beliefs which his parents adopted.

Then, the rationally basic criterion which any religion should fulfil to be regarded as rightful, will be pointed out. After that, historic events will be quickly mentioned, in which a debate took place between the Prophet of Islam (Muhammad, may Allah bless him and grant him peace) and the Jewish scholars about the truthfulness of Islam. A similar debate with the Christian scholars occurred and will also be mentioned.

The last section will discuss a side issue, nonetheless pivotal, which is that Prophet Ibrahim (may Allah grant him peace) did not belong to any faction. This clarification sets the basic concept that the Prophets were sent as a successive chain from God, and did not come with different goals or concepts. Only the practices in each religion were variable, but not the concept of the one God. This is crucial in order to comprehend, and hence believe, the purpose of the arrival of Prophet Muhammad (may Allah bless him and grant him peace).

3.1 One cannot go astray if he automatically follows the religion he found his parents practicing?

Every individual should realize that he will stand in front of God on Judgment day and talk to Him without the need for a translator.

The individual cannot have any person standing with him during judgement, he will be judged alone over his own choices. This necessitates that every person must make his own decisions in life regardless of what others think of him or lead him towards, because it is him that will bear the burden of those decisions alone.

Having said this, it is obvious that a person should carefully and personally research about the most important decision that will affect his life, both in this world and in the Hereafter, which is choosing his religion. Needless to say, what a person's parents chose as a religion should be an option and not a compulsion upon him to choose the same religion. This should be so, in spite of the tremendous favours they did for him, since they may be mistaken, and will be questioned individually by God on their own choices.

However, many people take the easy (or default) route and follow their parent's religion, because they are familiar and habituated to its rituals. Another factor is the emotional obstacle for them to consider that their parents followed the wrong religion, which would be too hurtful. Many individuals can't accept the idea that their parents were possibly astray in choosing their religion, and fall into the trap of following their parents, causing the same error to recur generation after generation.

But this is what God stresses upon to those people, for them to reflect upon this logically. '*When it is said to them: "Follow what Allah hath revealed" They say "Nay! We shall follow the ways of our fathers." What! Even though their fathers were void of wisdom and guidance?*' [2: 170][2]. This is the main issue: will they still follow their parents even if they lacked wisdom and righteousness?

The emphasis on what is wrong with that was shown in another verse, which contained a reply to those who used to have a strange ritual of exempting certain camels from human use. They did so in honour to their idols, claiming that God ordered them to do it. Additionally, they were very sceptic about changing those rituals.

God informed us about them *'When it is said to them: "Come to what Allah hath revealed; come to the Messenger": They say: "Enough for us are the ways we found our fathers following". What! Even though their fathers were void of knowledge and guidance?'* [5: 104][2]. In this verse, the term "knowledge" was used because they were accustomed to this habit rather than adopting it on the basis of authentic knowledge. If they traced it back, they would have found out that the origin of this absurd ritual was mere human fabrication.

So leaning on the excuse that it is convenient to follow one's parent's religion (blindly) is not a legitimate defence in front of God, and it is not worth the price that will be paid. And this response is a recurring one through each and every generation that were blessed with a Prophet; the same mistake which people keep falling into over and over again. God forewarns of this by saying:

And they have made the angels, who are servants of the Most Merciful, females. Did they witness their creation? Their testimony will be recorded, and they will be questioned. [19] And they said, "If the Most Merciful had willed, we would not have worshipped them." They have of that no knowledge. They are not but falsifying. [20] Or have We given them a book before the Qur'an to which they are adhering? [21] Rather, they say, "Indeed, we found our fathers upon a religion, and we are in their footsteps [rightly] guided." [22] And similarly, We did not send before you any warner into a city except that its affluent said, "Indeed, we found our fathers upon a religion, and we are, in their footsteps, following." [23] [Each warner] said, "Even if I brought you better guidance than that [religion] upon which you found your fathers?" They said, "Indeed we, in that with which you were sent, are disbelievers." [43: 19–24][1].

As a general principle, God denounces when some people claim that their sins are a fulfilment of God's will, i.e. that He ordered them to do so. God said *'And when they perform an obscenity, they say "We found our fathers (performing) it, and Allah has commanded us to (perform) it." Say: "Surely Allah does not command obscenity; do you say against*

Allah that which you do not know?" [7: 28][3]. On the contrary, this is what God commands: '*Indeed, Allah orders justice and good conduct and giving to relatives and forbids immorality and bad conduct and oppression. He admonishes you that perhaps you will be reminded.*' [16: 90][1].

So whether it is worshiping the idols that their fathers were worshipping, or having cultural habits such as mutilating parts of human (or animal) bodies as an alleged means of getting closer to God, or committing sins as drinking wine, this general principle applies. God is much higher and wiser than to order the performance of a detestable act.

3.2 The crucial basic criterion in any rightful religion

Once the concept of assessing a parent's religion before adopting it is fulfilled, the next logical question is: Then what is the 'right' religion that a person should follow? One thing is for certain, the correct religion must fulfil one basic criterion: that its carrier (messenger) must guide people to worship God, and not himself. If a human asks people to worship him, then it is for his own personal satisfaction and benefit, therefore it is not a rightful religion.

That being said, let's face ourselves frankly in order to emerge from this life safe. For an individual to find the truthful religion, he will have to investigate by himself. This requires effort, but that way he will be responsible for his own choices and will be certain of his religion through reasoning. More importantly, he will avoid falling victim to the influences of conniving liars, ignorant or arrogant people.

After this brief introduction, some background information is required before proceeding to the next section. It should be pointed out that Islam is a succession to Christianity, the same way Christianity is a succession to Judaism. So just as Christians believe in Moses and the apostles before him, Muslims believe in Jesus and Moses and the apostles before them (may Allah grant them peace). All of these religions guided people to worship one God, because all of those books came from the One God.

But the key problem is, in each religion there was a faction consisting of supposedly trusted religious figures (rabbis or priests) that hid or even altered some of the holy verses. Others twisted the meaning of the verses during translation or interpretation to distort the truth. For example, some rabbis concealed the verses that contained signs of the Prophet Jesus (may Allah grant him peace), who they were awaiting, and ended denying his prophecy. They did so under the pretence that he is not the awaited Messiah and they will await the actual one, and thus remained Jews, whilst the truthful Jews embraced Christianity.

The same happened to Prophet Muhammad (may Allah bless him and grant him peace) from some priests, hiding the signs that pointed to his identification, and stayed Christians. The rest recognized him and moved on to Islam. These Prophets are a succession to one another, in order to return people to the righteous path, and to deliver the complete message from God with all of its rules to people, in phases, throughout history.

So when Muhammad (may Allah bless him and grant him peace) came and invited Christians to follow him as their book says, the righteous Christians recognized him from his signs and from what he recites of what was revealed to him by God. *'And when they hear what has been revealed to the Messenger, you see their eyes overflowing with tears because of what they have recognized of the truth. They say,* *"Our Lord, we have believed, so register us among the witnesses"* [5: 83][1]. Consequently, they followed the Prophet.

Those Christians followed Muhammad once they ascertained he was the messenger that they were foretold of his arrival, because they faced themselves with an objective point. Their rationale was *'"And why should we not believe in Allah and what has come to us of the truth? And we aspire that our Lord will admit us [to Paradise] with the righteous people"* [5: 84][1]. So they pointed out: how can anyone expect to be admitted into Heaven with the righteous people if he does not follow the righteous path? This is especially true since they recognized that it is the righteous path, then what would become of them if they denied that it is so?

And Muhammad (may Allah bless him and grant him peace), being a successive (and the final) messenger in the chain of messengers, enlightened us about that. He said:

The similitude of mine and that of the Apostles before me is that of a person who built a house quite imposing and beautiful, but for one brick in one of its corners; people would go round it appreciating the building, but saying: Why has the brick not been fixed here? He (Muhammad, pbuh) said: I am that brick and I am the last of the Apostles.[12]

In the end, on judgment day, each religious faction (also known as: a nation) will follow its leader. So the true Jews will follow Moses, the true Christians will follow Jesus, and the true Muslims will follow Muhammad (may Allah bless the prophets and grant them peace). And so on regarding other religions and beliefs, so the Buddhists will follow Buddha, and the worshippers of fire will follow the fire.

Then, each Prophet will be a witness in front of God over his followers. And since Muhammad (may Allah bless him and grant him peace) is the last Prophet, not only will he be witness over Muslims, he will also be a witness over all the other Prophets whether they delivered God's message or not.

He will be a general witness over the leaders about whether they followed God's orders or not. Thus, for the true Prophets he will testify for them. This will be in contrast with other false leaders, who strayed and led people astray from the path of worshipping only God, like Buddha, and will testify against them.

He will testify for the true Prophets on the basis that Jews and Christians recognized and believed him when he came, and subsequently moved on to Islam. This is proof that the message was delivered thoroughly by the previous Prophets, so he witnesses for the previous Prophets in front of God that they did what they were ordered by God.

But what we should all be thinking about is what will our state be like when we, as followers, see this grand situation? And that is what God faces us with:

But how (will it be with them) when We bring of every people a witness, and We bring thee (O Muhammad) a witness against these? [41] On that day those who disbelieved and disobeyed the messenger will wish that they were level with the ground, and they can hide no fact from Allah. [4: 41–42][4].

God invokes our minds to ponder over this situation, so that those who are currently lying to themselves in this life and disbelieving out of stubbornness, or out of ease, may wake up and submit to the truth. This is because if they insist on following this path, they will wish that they get levelled with the ground (i.e. perish) rather than having to face this situation, and ultimately go through the reprisal that awaits them.

But neither will they perish nor will they be able to hide a single fact from God, the very same God who permitted their disbelief in Him. Their confession will include the reason which lured them to stay disbelievers, such as the desire to enjoy life to the fullest by committing sins freely, or to reach uniqueness and fame amidst people by being different. God will extract from them all their darkest thoughts and motives; what they concealed from everyone.

In conclusion, the main issues to verify are: whether Islam is from God or not, and whether Prophet Muhammad (may Allah bless him and grant him peace) was sincere in delivering it. This is what needs to be determined, and there are a few ways to verify these two issues, some have been mentioned whilst others will be mentioned.

3.3 A debate with the Jews

God ordered Prophet Muhammad (may Allah bless him and grant him peace) to present the Jews with a challenge to show who is being truthful, himself or them. It comes from Allah:

Say, [O Muhammad], "If the home of the Hereafter with Allah is for you alone and not the [other] people, then wish for death, if you should be truthful [94] But they will never wish for it, ever, because of what their hands have put forth. And Allah is knowing of the wrongdoers [95] And you will surely find them the most greedy of people for life [even] more than those who associate others with Allah. One of them wishes that he could be granted life a thousand years, but it would not remove him in the least from the [coming] punishment that he should be granted life. And Allah is seeing of what they do. [2: 94–96][1].

In the verses, God ordered Muhammad (may Allah bless him and grant him peace) to confront them with the discrepancy between their actions and their claims. This was presented as a challenge, that if they are honest in their claim that he isn't a Prophet and that Heaven is reserved for Jews only, then both parties should sit together and pray for death on the falsifying party.

It settled down that they abstained from doing so and eluded the confrontation. This leads to the conclusion that they knew that he was the true Prophet, since they ascertain that prayers of Prophets are definitely fulfilled from God. Yet, they insisted on staying Jews. And God informed us about how much they love life and fear death, on account of wishing to enjoy life pleasures to the maximum and loathing to be questioned upon their actions.

What is surprising is that they did this although they used to advise nonbelievers to believe in God, and ordered the sinners to do righteousness according to the holy book they had (Torah). Yet when the successive Prophets came, they disbelieved in them and resorted to immorality, such as lying about them or collaborating to murder them.

They wanted to evade being witnesses that those Prophets had the signs of the awaited Prophets, and to bury the revelations that would make their religion obsolete. This was practiced upon Muhammad just as they practiced it upon Jesus previously (peace be upon them).

We gave Moses the Book and followed him up with a succession of messengers; We gave Jesus the son of Mary Clear (Signs) and strengthened him with the holy spirit. Is it that whenever there comes to you a messenger with what ye yourselves desire not, ye are puffed up with pride?- Some ye called impostors, and others ye slay! [2: 87][5].

They ordered people to practice what they themselves did not practice, which is in fact hypocrisy, a feature which God greatly detests. God confronted them with this attitude of theirs also, for they may reflect upon their state and realize how astray they are. *'What! do you enjoin men to be good and neglect your own souls while you read the Book; have you then no sense?'* [2: 44][6].

They dismissed the fact that disbelieving in a true Prophet from God is still regarded as a disbelief in God. So in practicality, they picked the decrees they desired to follow and dismissed others, an act that God gravely warns from:

Then, you are those [same ones who are] killing one another and evicting a party of your people from their homes, cooperating against them in sin and aggression. And if they come to you as captives, you ransom them, although their eviction was forbidden to you. So do you believe in part of the Scripture and disbelieve in part? Then what is the recompense for those who do that among you except disgrace in worldly life; and on the Day of Resurrection they will be sent back to the severest of punishment. And Allah is not unaware of what you do. [2: 85][1].

All this yet they still consider themselves to be believers in God and followers of His laws. On that account, they convinced themselves that they deserve to be rewarded with Heaven, possibly after a brief period of punishment in Hell. They were harshly confronted with an uncontroversial fact:

And when it is said to them, "Believe in what Allah has revealed," they say, "We believe [only] in what was revealed to us." And they disbelieve in what came after it, while it is the truth confirming that which is with them. Say, "Then why did you kill the prophets of Allah before, if you are [indeed] believers?" [2: 91][1].

3.4 A debate with the Christians

Similarly, God ordered Prophet Muhammad (may Allah bless him and grant him peace) to confront the Christians about their statement that he isn't the awaited Prophet. This was done upon the fact that Jesus (may Allah grant him peace) is a Prophet, not God nor the son of God. He proposed that they should all gather and pray to God to curse the falsifying party about Jesus' nature.

God advised him saying *'Then whoever argues with you about it after [this] knowledge has come to you - say, "Come, let us call our sons and your sons, our women and your women, ourselves and yourselves, then supplicate earnestly [together] and invoke the curse of Allah upon the liars [among us]" [3: 61]*[1]; which they then evaded. And the logical argument that God bestowed upon Prophet Muhammad (may Allah bless him and grant him peace) was:

It is not for a human [prophet] that Allah should give him the Scripture and authority and prophethood and then he would say to the people, "Be servants to me rather than Allah" but [instead, he would say], "Be pious scholars of the Lord because of what you have taught of the Scripture and because of what you have studied." [79] Nor could he order you to take the angels and prophets as lords. Would he order you to disbelief after you had been Muslims? [3: 79–80][1] (Muslims meaning: people who submitted to God's orders; and Muslim in Arabic literally means a person who submits).

This is a very logical question, how is it befitting to Jesus (may Allah grant him peace) that he leads his followers into blasphemy after he had led them to submit to the word of God!? So the truth is, Jesus (may Allah grant him peace) didn't order his followers to worship him, but the scholars after him portrayed to the people that Jesus should be worshipped.

3.5 Factions claimed that Prophet Ibrahim (may Allah grant him peace) belonged to its faction

There are Jews who claimed that Prophet Ibrahim (may Allah grant him peace) was a Jew, while some Christians claimed that he was a Christian, so the question is what faction did he really belong to? More accurately stated, what were his beliefs? The answer came in the Quran with a very logical point *'O people of the Scripture (Jews and Christians)! Why do you dispute about Ibrahim (Abraham), while the Taurat (Torah) and the Injeel (Gospel) were not revealed till after him? Have you then no sense? [65] Verily, you are those who have disputed about that of which you have knowledge. Why do you then dispute concerning that which you have no knowledge? It is Allah Who knows, and you know not.'* [3: 65-66][2].

So, the truth that is revealed to us in the Quran is that he was neither Jew nor Christian, since the Torah and the Bible came after him. Furthermore, this was followed by another refute from God. This was in the fact that they argued rightfully with people, out of knowledge, about what was truthful (the beneficial and harmful matters to humans according to the scriptures, in the form of permissible and forbidden); but why unrightfully argue about what they have no knowledge about, since they didn't witness Prophet Ibrahim (may Allah grant him peace).

What Ibrahim believed, like all the other Prophets, is that there is only one God, and he termed anyone who believed that to be "Muslim" (i.e. a person who submitted to the one God). And hence it is where Muslims get their title, for we don't claim that he belongs to our faction, but as a matter of fact it is the other way round. It is us who belong to his faction, and the faction of all the other Prophets, because all the Prophets had the same belief. The last of these Prophets was Muhammad (may Allah bless him and grant him peace), who implemented this title for his followers.

In conclusion, a very smart and practical inquiry remains to be answered. The inquiry is: If Islam is the rightful religion to follow, then why is the state of many Muslim societies so underdeveloped in terms of economic, scientific, social, political standards, etc.?

The answer, shamefully and painfully to admit, is that many Muslims don't abide by the Islamic laws in their daily interactions and conduct. This is especially apparent in interactions containing a financial aspect. The logical point that we as Muslims should face ourselves with is: Why should God honour a nation that doesn't abide by His laws!?

If we don't recognize, admit and face ourselves with this existent flaw, how do we expect to amend it and improve? After all, Islam encourages a person to be honest, which entitles being frank (and moreover judging) with oneself. The flaw is within us Muslims and not in Islam itself, but it reflects upon Islam in the eyes of non-Muslims. This is the concise answer.

That being said, irrespective of what religion a person eventually settles upon (although being the most important issue to decide upon in a person's life), there is one acknowledged principle. This common principle, which no faction that believes in God can argue with, is that God is not to be disobeyed. This will be discussed in the next chapter.

Chapter 4: Abusing the fact that God is forgiving

After a person has settled upon a religion that he will embrace (after assessing it, finding logic and peace within it), there is one common denominator that all should meet upon. This common denominator is that a person should never take disobeying God lightly, for it is illogical to assume that one can do what God dislikes and yet be rewarded with what the individual would like from Him (i.e. Heaven).

Since a believer knows that God created many of His creatures with a basic feature, sight, he must keep in mind that God has that feature too before performing anything questionable *'Does he not know that Allah sees?'* [96: 14][1]. However, God's sight is far superior to that of all whom He created, for He observes everyone, everywhere, at the same instant.

Nonetheless, some believers try to swindle around this fact when sinning, deviously depending on His mercy, kindness and forgiveness. Here are some widespread excuses that people resort to, but which Allah had refuted:

4.1 We are special to God, so we will be forgiven!

This line of thought is one of the major delusions that a group from every religious faction strays from the path with. This is because people generally are prone to believing the dream that they can do whatever they want on Earth and still be rewarded from God with Heaven in the Hereafter. They believe so because they wish for it to be true, that it is possible to enjoy the test –life– and enjoy the Hereafter; enjoyment over enjoyment, which is illogical. And the reality of the matter is: if someone is desperate enough to believe in something, he will believe it with the slightest suggestion or vaguest signal.

Relating between what was just mentioned and the subject of this book, currently many Jews do whatever sins they please on account that they will be forgiven because they are special to God. They claim speciality on the ground that they relate to Israel (who is Jacob, may Allah grant him peace), whilst some moreover assert that Ezra is the son of God whom they follow.

Meanwhile, many Christians act the same way based on the claim that Jesus (may Allah grant him peace) is the son of God whom they follow, and his crucifixion pays for their sins. Building upon that assumption, which is that both factions are unaccountable for their sins, then the continual of their test on Earth would be pointless. Practicality speaking, in that case scenario they have all passed the test already and should be transferred to Heaven. Yet, the test is still taking place, which conflicts with these presumptions.

And similarly, many Muslims misconceive that because they believe in only one God that they are safe, and they will be exempted from entering Hell, which is not true. This is because believing in one God (Allah) prevents a Muslim from residing in Hell *eternally*. If a Muslim commits injustices and sins, he will have to atone for them by entering Hell in the Hereafter even though he believes in Allah alone. And this is God's justice, that whomever does injustices to His creatures (including animals) must be punished for it, regardless of what he believes in. This is the main rule that is enacted upon all beings.

When Prophet Muhammad (may Allah bless him and grant him peace) came, he invited the Jews and Christians to enter Islam but they refused. This necessitated that he warns them from the consequences of not following the message of God. Ultimately, they claimed that God will not punish them because they are special to Him and are followers of His sons.

When this happened, God bestowed upon Muhammad (may Allah bless him and grant him peace) a rationale to present to them, one that was logical and will ultimately discredit their excuse. He said:

And (both) the Jews and the Christians say: "We are the children of Allah and His loved ones." Say: "Why then does He punish you for your sins?" Nay, you are but human beings, of those He has created, He forgives whom He wills and He punishes whom He wills. And to Allah belongs the dominion of the heavens and the earth and all that is between them, and to Him is the return (of all). [5: 18][2].

And this is very sensible, that if they were really special then why did they get punished on Earth, such as having pests sent on them or get banished from Jerusalem? Even in modern time they get sick, get hit by storms, and fall victims to injustices from others. Some people may say these are natural occurrences, but does anyone deny that God can prevent a misfortune from befalling upon a person if He wills to protect that person? The truth is: a misfortune cannot befall a person except if God ultimately permits it (and the same for good fortune).

So this is the fact that every human must know, that disobeying God's orders deserves punishment from Him, no matter how special or unique that person is. And the reality is, whoever obeys God is the special one to Him, and whoever disobeys Him is one whom God discontents.

Prophet Muhammad (may Allah bless him and grant him peace) reminds us of a basic fact, and advises us upon it. He said:

O people, verily your Lord is One and your father [Adam] is one. Verily there is no favour of an Arab over a foreigner, or of a foreigner over an Arab, or of a red man over a black man, or of a black man over a red man, except in terms of piety. Have I conveyed the message?[13]

He further stresses that a person's value lies in the purity of his heart (intentions) and his deeds. He said:

Verily, Allah does not look to your faces and your wealth, but He looks to your heart and to your deeds.[14]

Nonetheless, some people still insist on disobeying God and sinning as they please on account that they are unique from others, so God questions them about a phenomenon which they can verify by themselves. He says:

Have they not seen how many generations We destroyed before them which We had established upon the earth as We have not established you? And We sent [rain from] the sky upon them in showers and made rivers flow beneath them; then We destroyed them for their sins and brought forth after them a generation of others. [6: 6][1].

He states this warningly to them and requests them to use their minds regarding what they observe, on account that they may stop their stubbornness and submit to the truth. There were generations before us that were exiled from their lands, invaded by other nations or got hit by catastrophes. This occurred despite their claims that they believed in God, and despite the fact that He used to bestow His blessings upon them amply. All this did not avail them from being punished for their grave sins, and they were overcome by God's power despite their unique advancement.

But alas, many people have paired between two, individually demising, features: taking God's laws lightly, and taking for granted that punishment will not strike them personally. This is an issue which God addresses:

Do ye feel secure that He Who is in heaven will not cause you to be swallowed up by the earth when it shakes (as in an earthquake)? [16] Or do ye feel secure that He Who is in Heaven will not send against you a violent tornado (with showers of stones), so that ye shall know how (terrible) was My warning? [17] But indeed men before them rejected (My warning): then how (terrible) was My rejection (of them)? [67: 16–18][5].

And this is a very inciting point, that how are we so confident that God will not punish us for disobeying Him while living upon His Earth and under His skies? Shouldn't a person who wishes to continuously disobey God firstly try to live on a land that does not belong to God?

Additionally, there is a misconception to many people that committing sins takes its toll in the Hereafter only, i.e. Hell. However, this is a very deceitful mirage, because sins are detrimental to a person in this life as well.

Many people do not know that God forbade matters upon us because they are harmful to us, or because their harm exceeds their benefits. However, God promises of a punishment from Him upon doing these things to increase our repulsion from them. Consider this situation as with the laws within a community. We all know that stealing and killing is wrong and detrimental to the community, but if the law didn't criminalize and punish people over it, crime rates would skyrocket.

Since these forbidden things harm us, it is without a doubt that committing them takes a toll on the human body and the human mind. The burden on the human body is, for example, how alcohol impairs brain functionality and causes liver damage. The burden on the human mind is how adultery causes emotional scarring to people. These physical and mental burdens accumulate in the human body, more profoundly so if someone commits multiple sins and very frequently. The negative effects then cause the person to feel unstable or frustrated or depressed, even if it is not apparent or understandable to people.

In the end, these burdens become so overwhelming that the person 'feels' that something is gravely wrong but cannot identify it, and if they persist and become heavy enough, he may start to think about suicide. What proves this point is that in certain advanced countries the ratio of suicides is very high, although those that commit suicide may have everything at their disposal, such as abundant money and peace and freedom of intercourse.

They do everything that they desire, yet at the end of the day they feel unhappy, so why is that? On the other hand, many third world countries have low suicide rates, but how is this the case?

This although one would expect it to be the other way around, in that people in advanced countries with luxurious lives wouldn't want to commit suicide, and would rather enjoy their luxury. Meanwhile, it is expected that people in third world countries with tough lives would want to escape from it via suicide. The truth is that rich people are able to and do commit more sins, and are therefore usually farther from God, while poor people are less capable of committing sins. Poorer people have limitations as to how far they can sin, due to financial restrictions and reduced free time for example.

More so of notice, although people that have everything at their disposal can do as they please, yet they feel 'unsatisfied' because they weren't designed for that by God. They were not created nor designed to spend their lives chasing their bodily desires. He designed us to find spiritual comfort in worshipping Him, resorting to Him and connecting with Him. Our desires are but a temptation to us which we should control and refine.

In summation, the point to be made is that who sin a lot feel 'choked', a suffocating like feeling. And this is what God indicated about, with a very accurate and expressive description, in the following verse to point out what do those who disobey Him feel like:

And [He also forgave] the three who were left behind [and regretted their error] to the point that the earth closed in on them in spite of its vastness and their souls confined them, and they were certain that there is no refuge from Allah except in Him. Then He turned to them so they could repent. Indeed, Allah is the Accepting of repentance, the Merciful [9:118][1].

In this verse, God informs us about what three people who did a grave disobedience felt like. They felt like that from guilt and being distanced from God, and when they asked for repentance truthfully,

God bestowed His forgiveness upon them. The point to be made is that for a person who keeps sinning (even if he doesn't believe in God), guilt and burdens keep accumulating inside of him, because this is how God designed man when encountering sins.

Therefore, many individuals who think about suicide have been struck by this inexpressible frustrating feeling, somewhat like being strangulated and yet being helpless about it. And only a person who is lost and has experienced this feeling previously will fully comprehend what this verse is describing.

4.2 The pretence that a person cannot be doing something wrong since God allows it.

There is a common excuse which a group of people use to justify their disobedience, and that is on the grounds that if what they were doing is wrong then God would've prevented it. This line of thought is a result of faulty reasoning combined with stubbornness, and is denounced in the Quran:

And those who associate others with Allah say, "If Allah had willed, we would not have worshipped anything other than Him, neither we nor our fathers, nor would we have forbidden anything through other than Him." Thus did those do before them. So is there upon the messengers except [the duty of] clear notification? [16: 35][1].

However, this excuse is not confined within polytheists alone, rather it is utilized by a segment in every belief faction to disobey God. This concept is flawed from multiple perspectives, and the stated verse presents logical replies which annul this excuse. One reply is that the Prophets are responsible only in delivering the message, and actually have no authority of forcing it upon someone. This emphasizes that belief is a matter of choice, meaning that a human is free to go against God's will and disbelieve in His message.

Those who use this excuse omit the crucial fact that God allows humans to go against His will on Earth, since this is a test. Thus, our ability to perform something is not a valid indicator that God is content with it, and hence should not be used as an expedient to disobey God. What pleases God or what He detests is stated in His messages, and that is the source from which we should learn about what He wills.

Another reply embedded in the verse is that monotheism exists, and by assuming their same reasoning it means that God willed its presence and He is pleased by it. But monotheism and polytheism are contradictory, which indicates that the mere presence of a belief system isn't an indicator of its rightfulness or that it pleases God. Thus this proves that there is a flaw in their reasoning. There is a difference between what God wills and what He loves, for He may will the presence of something which He hates, to test us.

The error in their reasoning arises from ignorance that God's will is categorized into two classes: Universal and Legislative. The universal will, such as causing rain and in what quantity, or the features of a person when he is born, is a will in which we have no control over and indifferently befalls. This will cannot be defied or altered. On the other hand, God's legislative will consists of the rules He places which we are supposed to follow, but He granted us the ability to defy them, upon which we will be recompensed accordingly. The problem is that some people picture God's universal will with the foundations of God's legislative will.

In practical life, the discrepancy in such individuals' claims becomes overly apparent when they struggle to achieve a benefit, or to lift a misfortune that hit them. Since it is God's will that they have a job that doesn't pay well, or have an illness which burdens them, why then do they try to improve their status? Furthermore, when they strive to commit a sin, what is the explanation in this case? Does committing a sin actually mean that God is satisfied with it? All these points indicate that either they wrongfully understand God's will, or that they are applying a double standard (based upon their desires) in judging matters. Either way, they contradict their reasoning and invalidate their credibility.

4.3 The audacious concept that one may disobey God and will reside in Hell for only a few days

God says to those who distorted the previous holy books to hide the truth '*And they say, "Never will the Fire touch us, except for a few days." Say, "Have you taken a covenant with Allah? For Allah will never break His covenant. Or do you say about Allah that which you do not know?"* [2: 80][1]. This is a threatening inquisition for such criminals to think about. The warning is directed even to those who don't distort verses in holy books but are corrupt in their actions, convincing themselves that they will bear the few days they spend in Hell.

All such audacious people should confront themselves, did they personally take an oath from God that He will not leave them in Hell except for a few days? Then the question remains: how can they be so confident that this will be the case with them, in spite of the fact that they have disobeyed Him so gravely? And on a side note, even if they do spend just a few days in the best case scenario, Hell is so severe that even those few days in the black roaring fire will be enough to revoke all that they enjoyed on Earth. For no one can outsmart God.

Moreover, God asks people who act and think like that a logical question for them to contemplate upon, '*How (will it be) when We gather them together on the Day about which there is no doubt (i.e. the Day of Resurrection), and each person will be paid in full what he has earned? And they will not be dealt with unjustly*' [3: 25][2]. Indeed, when these people are fairly fulfilled a verdict based on the crimes they committed, do they still see they deserve just a few days in Hell?

Undoubtedly, they need to revise their assessments and their actions; undoubtedly, they are being arrogant. It is an arrogance that will be the doom of them. An arrogance accompanied by smugness whose source is puzzling, especially when God detests such a characteristic on account of how weak and miniscule we are in the Universe.

Yet indeed again, they need to revise their actions, how they audaciously take His mercy and forgiveness for granted, abusing them. This while God has not granted them an immunity from Him. In fact, He warned people from defying Him, and reminds us all of what He did to previous civilizations that defied His rules (such as the Pharaohs who had reached great power and advancements, yet were wiped out):

Did the people of the towns feel secure against the coming of Our wrath by night while they were asleep? [97] Or else did they feel secure against its coming in broad daylight while they played about (care-free)? [98] Did they then feel secure against the plan of Allah?- but no one can feel secure from the Plan of Allah, except those (doomed) to ruin! [99] To those who inherit the earth in succession to its (previous) possessors, is it not a guiding, (lesson) that, if We so willed, We could punish them (too) for their sins, and seal up their hearts so that they could not hear? [7: 97–100][2].

Overall, committing sins freely on account that God will forgive is practically being conniving with God, since the person intends to do what God detests and yet expects to use the argument that He is forgiving against Him. This line of irrational reasoning is usually concealed by those who believe in it, but God forewarns them that He knows what they conceal or reveal to their close peers alike: *'Did they not know that Allah knows their secrets and their private conversations and that Allah is the Knower of the unseen?' [9: 78]*[1].

This includes knowing the conversations they have within themselves to reach the justification for eluding righteousness. Wishing for God's forgiveness should be accompanied by expending effort to please Him, if a person is to be truthful and logical with himself.

4.4 Is it fair that God equates between the pious and the mischievous during reward?

For the sake of conclusiveness, let's assume that it does happen that those wrongdoers will be forgiven because they are special. In other words, the atrocious criminals last only a few days in Hell, after which they are allowed to enter Heaven. How then will it be fair if the evil people and the pious people, who abided by God's laws, end up in the same place eventually? God asks us *'Shall We then treat the People of Faith like the People of Sin? [35] What is the matter with you? How judge ye?'* [68: 35–36][2].

The truth is, it can't happen, because that will be unfair to those who worked hard obeying God, and as mentioned before, God is fair with His creations to the utmost level. Being equalled in the Hereafter would be similar to a student who studied very hard for an exam and barely passes, while another student who played all year long and didn't study barely passes too in the same exam.

The reality of the situation is that Heaven consists of ranks, where each ascending rank is superior in terms of enjoyment and closeness to God. So from those who sinned a lot and eventually enter Heaven (which will certainly never happen for the disbelievers and those who fought God's messengers), they will be in the lowest level in Heaven. So this is the best case scenario for the sinners, because if they got other than that it wouldn't be fair to those who strived to obey God and evaded defying Him.

And so they won a bit on Earth by doing all that they wanted, but will get the weakest pleasures in the Hereafter that is eternal, which is an overall tremendous loss when compared to the pious. God's justice is much more precise than to equate between the two groups in the Hereafter, and He draws our attention to this fact in general by saying:

Is one who is obedient to Allah, prostrating himself or standing (in prayer) during the hours of the night, fearing the Hereafter and hoping for the Mercy of his Lord (like one who disbelieves)? Say: "Are those who know equal to those who know not?" It is only men of understanding who will remember (i.e. get a lesson from Allah's Signs and Verses). [39: 9][2].

Then, God makes clear the difference between the pious and the corrupt by resembling them to the difference between Heaven and Hell. This is an indication that the difference between them is the same as the difference between their destinies in the Hereafter. God gives us this beautiful and logical similitude:

Is he who is on a clear proof from his Lord, like those for whom their evil deeds that they do are beautified for them, while they follow their own lusts (evil desires)? [14] The description of Paradise which the Muttaqun (pious) have been promised is that in it are rivers of water the taste and smell of which are not changed; rivers of milk of which the taste never changes; rivers of wine delicious to those who drink; and rivers of clarified honey (clear and pure), therein for them is every kind of fruit; and forgiveness from their Lord. (Are these) like those who shall dwell forever in the Fire, and be given, to drink, boiling water, so that it cuts up their bowels? [47: 14–15][2].

4.5 Following the devil brings about great worldly benefits?

Generally speaking, this concept is of high truthfulness, that forsaking one's obligation of obeying God and abandoning honourable morals will very likely lead a person to great materialistic worldly gains. But a person should ask himself: at what cost? The cost is earning God's detestation and hence deserving punishment, to obtain fortune, fame, authority or beautiful companions. What's more discouraging is that all of these worldly decorations will inevitably be left behind at death. Hence, a person wouldn't be able to make full use of them; they just don't last. God informs us:

And whatever you have been given is an enjoyment of the life of (this) world and its adornment, and that (Hereafter) which is with Allah is better and will remain forever. Have you then no sense? [60] Is he whom We have promised an excellent promise (Paradise), which he will find true, like him whom We have made to enjoy the luxuries of the life of (this) world, then on the Day of Resurrection, he will be among those brought up (to be punished in the Hell-fire)? [28: 60–61][2].

Anyone who follows the devil will lose his value as a person, but more importantly will lose his Hereafter with God. That person has sold his long and luxurious future in order to immediately gain the short and inferior present, for God promises us the Hereafter while the devil promises us prosperity according to earthly standards.

This happens because when someone takes the devil as his companion, then God usually opens the doors of these earthly goods upon that individual. God does so because the Earth, with all that's in it, is worth nothing to Him, which the disbeliever sells his soul for. However, God questions us about the rationale of such a decision:

And [mention] when We said to the angels, "Prostrate to Adam," and they prostrated, except for Iblees (Satan). He was of the jinn and departed from the command of his Lord. Then will you take him and his descendants as allies other than Me while they are enemies to you? Wretched it is for the wrongdoers as an exchange. [50] I did not make them witness to the creation of the heavens and the earth or to the creation of themselves, and I would not have taken the misguiders as assistants. [18: 50–51][1].

Is it logical for anyone to take his enemy as a friend or advisor? Our father Adam (may Allah grant him peace) did it once out of inexperience and trusted Satan's promise of superiority if he eats from the tree, so have we forgotten what was the consequence of that?

We have been banished from Heaven and sent to live on this Earth as a test, after Adam (may Allah grant him peace) disobeyed God and ate from the tree. The next time any of us trusts Satan, he will be evicted from this Earth and sent to Hell instead of returning to Heaven. And to those who not only befriend and follow the devil but also worship him, is it logical that someone who did not witness the creation of the Skies and the Earth, or even the creation of mankind, deserves to be worshipped?

Finally, there is a very risky aspect to this path to an extent that a sensible person would avoid it. What if the person sells all his morals to the devil in order to obtain great worldly success, but yet he doesn't receive it? What will be his state when he misses the rewards in the world and also loses the rewards in the Hereafter for following the immoral path? How is investing all of a person's valuables with someone untrustworthy a wise decision?

In summary to this chapter, the main principle to be delivered is that there is no legitimate excuse for a believer to wilfully commit a sin which he knows that God prohibited. Whether this is under the presumption that he himself is unique from others, that the case in this incident is different, or any other pretence, it is unacceptable and moreover logically refuted.

However, this is not the only issue which is addressed logically in regards to believers. Some people may imagine that belief in God is based purely on faith, but in Islam it is reinforced with a logical aspect. In the next chapter, it will be apparent that logical arguments are provided, to those who already believed in Allah, in moral issues and even some decreed laws. This is because understanding the wisdom behind the rules strengthens the faith of believers.

Chapter 5: Logical concepts for Muslims

Believing in Allah is the mental aspect of faith. However, this mental aspect should manifest itself in the actions of the believer, otherwise there would be no practical difference between believers and disbelievers. In that scenario, believers would not have integrity nor truthfulness, since an aspect of integrity and truthfulness is following through with what you believe. Logical perspectives are presented to Muslims to motivate them more in following through with the laws.

Thus, a believer is under constant development in both: his principles and his actions; for his progression has not ended just by acknowledging the presence of Allah. Here are some logical concepts that are presented to Muslims, which they should come to terms with:

5.1 Heaven is not cheap

Some of those who believe in Allah wonder: why am I still being hit by heavy hardships although I believe in Allah? That believer may moreover be pious and infrequently disobeys Allah, expecting to have a calm and easy life for that. But the key issue is that this perspective is incomplete.

The main reason that hardships befall disbelievers is because they are walking blindly in the journey of life, thus tripping and crashing into walls. It is like a tourist roaming a country without a guide; someone who hasn't read the operation manual about himself regarding what harms him as a human being. However, believers also must pass through hardships in order to be tried and ranked by Allah:

Do the people think that they will be left to say, "We believe" and they will not be tried? [2] But We have certainly tried those before them, and Allah will surely make evident those who are truthful, and He will surely make evident the liars. [3] Or do those who do evil deeds think they can outrun Us? Evil is what they judge. [29: 2–4][1].

Moreover, since their destiny is Heaven, there must be a price for it, since something so valuable cannot come at a cheap price. Declaring belief without proving it through actions would be like wanting a free membership to a unique organization; if many could enter it easily, it would lose some of its uniqueness.

On that account, Allah consoles the believers about the hardships they still have to face. Why should a party of believers receive special treatment from the others by passing through life without hardships, when there are those who were threatened and then killed for believing in Allah? Those people did not disbelieve to save their lives. Others fought back till they reached exhaustion, up to the point of desperately awaiting Allah's victory to them:

Or do you think that you will enter Paradise while such [trial] has not yet come to you as came to those who passed on before you? They were touched by poverty and hardship and were shaken until [even their] messenger and those who believed with him said,"When is the help of Allah?" Unquestionably, the help of Allah is near. [2: 214][1].

How can there be those who were tested so rigorously about their faith, whilst we expect to pass life with just being lightly tested?

5.2 Doing sins due to pressure from people, or being tempted by them, is not a legitimate excuse to Allah.

Some believers will lean towards sinning due to reasons related to people, such as being intimidated or criticized by people, or being allured due to the large number of people committing a particular sin. However, this is not a practical excuse in front of Allah, and Prophet Saleh (peace be upon him) reached a logical conclusion regarding this matter. He stated '*He said, "O my people, have you considered: if I should be upon clear evidence from my Lord and He has given me mercy from*

Himself, who would protect me from Allah if I disobeyed Him? So you would not increase me except in loss.' [11: 63][1].

The fact is, no matter how many or how influential a person is, their numbers and statuses mean nothing in front of a violation of Allah's laws. No one, not a single one, from the elites or all these masses of people can protect you from Allah's wrath. Nor will anyone dare to take the heat for your sins and bear your burdens in the Hereafter, even if he personally pushed you to do it and is directly responsible.

No one will risk his own safety by acting as a shield for someone else in front of Allah, not even between relatives or loved ones. In fact, using people as an excuse in front of Allah may make a person's situation worse, since it may mean that he disobeyed Allah to please people, so who is more important to such an individual and who should he have feared more?

5.3 Who will argue for a deviant peer on judgement day?

It is of chivalry and loyalty to help a brother/relative/friend in a critical situation, and these are features that Allah commends. But the question is: can we do this up to what extent? If a best friend gets done an injustice, or is afflicted by a disaster, it is essential that he be helped; but what if he stole someone and is evading being captured? Should a person hide him from the authorities or help him escape punishment?

Here is where the line is drawn. If a peer commits a violation intentionally, he should be advised and scolded, even hired a lawyer to defend him, but never assisted in completing or getting away with his crime. This crime that he committed afflicted someone anonymous, and on the social level, justice in this scenario is more important than presumed chivalry. Aiding a peer in inflicting harm on someone is not chivalry, it is a false chivalry since it is on the expense of an innocent creature. On the contrary, aiding a thief evade capture is the same as aiding him in the theft itself, since his theft cannot be completed if he does not evade the authorities with his stolen property.

But let's stay with this scenario till the presumably best ending for the peer: that his friends hide him and argue for him till he escapes and isn't punished. According to Allah's justice, he still didn't pay for his crime, and thus will be judged upon it in the Hereafter and will be made to pay for it. The question then is, who will dare risking his own well-being and argue against Allah for his stray peer? Where will chivalry be then? Is it loyalty to help a peer evade punishment in this world only to leave him face an even greater punishment for it in the Hereafter without defending him?

This exact situation occurred with a group people at the era of the Prophet (may Allah bless him and grant him peace). But this was what Allah confronted them with *'Here you are - those who argue on their behalf in [this] worldly life - but who will argue with Allah for them on the Day of Resurrection, or who will [then] be their representative?'* [4: 109][1]. Thus a general rule has been set, a Muslim is required to stand by his brother, unless an injustice has been done. At that point, aiding his brother involves advising him to do the right thing, and preventing his harm from reaching others.

5.4 Good deeds can be annulled by detestable deeds

Believers should not reach the point of boasting about their good deeds; but in fact, they should have humbleness as their feature. That is because boasting is detested by Allah, and may even contaminate good deeds to the point of annulling them by His standards. For example, regarding those who do a good deed to show off to people, how can they expect to be rewarded for it from Allah when it wasn't intended for Allah in the first place?

Another example is a person who gives charity, but tells the needy person to remember that he did him a favour, or harms him in another way. Such deeds appear good, but have been poisoned by foul intentions or opposing actions. Allah gives a similitude about such deeds:

Would one of you like to have a garden of palm trees and grapevines underneath which rivers flow in which he has from every fruit? But he is afflicted with old age and has weak offspring, and it is hit by a whirlwind containing fire and is burned. Thus does Allah make clear to you [His] verses that you might give thought. [2: 266][1].

Allah portrays how a person who has a beautiful garden with rivers flowing through it is unable to benefit from it when he needed it the most: when he aged and has children depending on him. Similarly, he who poisons his good deeds will be unable to reap its fruits when he needs it the most: in the Hereafter.

5.5 Why doesn't Allah guide all the people to Him?

A logical inquiry that believers may wonder upon is why doesn't Allah guide all the people to recognizing, acknowledging and worshiping Him? In other words, why aren't the signs of His existence indisputably clear? This way, everyone will enter Heaven and no one will suffer in Hell.

It must be firstly pointed that Allah's signs are already very clear: the Sun, Moon, stars, seas, plants, animals and rain are all signs of Allah's existence. It is just that many people have grown accustomed to these wonders. Allah has even sent Holy books and numerous Prophets to guide people and inform them about Him, effectively eliminating any excuse for disbelief. He did everything other than revealing Himself directly to us:

Indeed, We have revealed to you, [O Muhammad], as We revealed to Noah and the prophets after him. And we revealed to Abraham, Ishmael, Isaac, Jacob, the Descendants, Jesus, Job, Jonah, Aaron, and Solomon, and to David We gave the book [of Psalms]. [163] And [We sent] messengers about whom We have related [their stories] to you before and messengers about whom We have not related to you. And Allah spoke to Moses with [direct] speech. [164] [We sent] messengers as bringers of good tidings and warners so that mankind will have no argument against Allah after the messengers. And ever is Allah Exalted in Might and Wise. [4: 163–165][1].

He didn't reveal Himself directly otherwise everyone would believe in Him without exception, which wouldn't distinguish arrogant individuals from the rest. The aim of testing us is to demonstrate who is overly prideful to the extent of rejecting Allah's existence when presented with just indirect signs about His existence.

But why is this test, which will result in some people ending in Hell eternally, necessary in the first place? This is because Allah had already created angels, creatures who have no free will and cannot disobey Him. It was Allah's will to create species that have the ability to disobey Him, moreover disbelieve in Him if they wished. The wisdom behind this is that whomever worships Allah upon free will is a much more advanced and elite creature than those who worship Allah by default. Thus it was Allah's will to create a far more sophisticated and potentially unique creature than angels.

On this line of thought, some believers may reach a more critical and complex question: If Allah foreknowingly knew that most people would enter Hell, why did He create them in the first place when He knew that they would eternally suffer? The answer is contained within this verse '*How shall Allah guide a people who disbelieved after their belief and had witnessed that the Messenger is true and clear signs had come to them? And Allah does not guide the wrongdoing people.*' [3: 86][1].

This is a very logical perspective, one that answers directly and indirectly all the questions in this section. If someone sees all the indirect signs about Allah's existence and identifies a messenger as being truly sent from Him, yet chooses to disbelieve in Allah, what more is required to satisfy him? It's obviously not an issue about what signs that person needs anymore, it's an issue of what he wants to do. Why should Allah guide such a person then, when that person himself does not desire to be guided?

This point is what many thinkers overlook, that although Allah foreknows what each person's fate will be and that there will be casualties from this test, He never forced anyone into disbelief or becoming harmful to living creatures. Every human has free will after all, but there are individuals who desire to stay astray and forge their own paths in falsehood. We needed to see this to believe it, and that is why this test is undergoing instead of Allah sending us to our fate without giving every one of us the chance on a practical field (Earth). To that extent is Allah's graciousness and justice.

5.6 Being a Muslim means I should be concerned only about myself?

After accepting belief, one should not go down the path that he reached safety now and should be concerned about only his own safety. This is a very passive and corruption-spreading line of thought, since a passive Muslim is a weak Muslim who doesn't help living creatures in dire situations. If Islam is the rightful religion and the truth from Allah, then it would be expected from it to order its followers upon aiding justice on Earth in general, even between non-Muslims, which it does.

If a non-Muslim nation commits genocide or is discriminatory against another non-Muslim nation that cries for help, are we supposed to let that injustice befall others just because it isn't related to us? How would the rightful religion from Allah allow, or even just ignore, the oppression of anyone from whom He created irrespective of what his belief is? And that is exactly what is dealt with in this verse:

And what is [the matter] with you that you fight not in the cause of Allah and [for] the oppressed among men, women, and children who say, "Our Lord, take us out of this city of oppressive people and appoint for us from Yourself a protector and appoint for us from Yourself a helper?" [4: 75][1].

Islam is a religion of justice, and fighting to establish justice is still regarded by Allah as fighting for His cause. Thus, it is not an option for us to passively watch tyrants as they overtake weaker individuals/ nations; this is not an attribute of ours.

5.7 Belief in Allah should not be forced upon anyone

A common misconception among some Muslims is that they should make non-Muslims become Muslims even if by compulsion if necessary. However, this concept is wrong, as indicated in some verses such as this *'And had your Lord willed, those on earth would have believed - all of them entirely. Then, [O Muhammad], would you compel the people in order that they become believers?'* [10: 99][1].

This depicts that Allah's wisdom behind placing humans on Earth is not to make them all accept belief in Him, rather it is to see those who choose to believe in Him when given the ability to disbelieve in Him. The core argument is, if the main target from placing humans on Earth is a situation in which everyone would be Muslims, Allah would have done it Himself. Since Allah Himself bestowed upon man the freedom to disbelieve in Him, what right do we have to take away the right of choice from individuals.

Forcing a belief upon someone would make him declare it, but secretly his heart won't accept it, practically forcing the person into becoming a hypocrite. More importantly, Allah will not accept this person's good actions since he does not believe in Allah with his heart, which is a prerequisite for good deeds to be accepted. Thus the end result would be pointlessness, since the person will declare Islam but will not actually practice nor benefit from it.

Such a person did not believe in Allah due to a problem in his heart, so forcefully becoming a Muslim still doesn't fix the main issue:

his heart. Such people, due to their bad hearts and consequently their evil deeds, Allah does not will to guide them into accepting Islam, so how can we make Islam enter their hearts when Allah and themselves don't want that? And this is what Allah brings us to terms with:

What is [the matter] with you [that you are] two groups concerning the hypocrites, while Allah has made them fall back [into error and disbelief] for what they earned. Do you wish to guide those whom Allah has sent astray? And he whom Allah sends astray - never will you find for him a way [of guidance]. [4: 88][1].

Furthermore, forcing Islam upon someone will possibly make him resent Islam more, making the situation worse than what it was. As for the Muslims who still insist on forcing Islam upon people, under the presumption of convincing them of the truth for example by time, Allah informs us that the Quran in itself is powerful enough upon truth-seekers. He says:

And if there was any qur'an by which the mountains would be removed or the earth would be broken apart or the dead would be made to speak, [it would be this Qur'an], but to Allah belongs the affair entirely. Then have those who believed not accepted that had Allah willed, He would have guided the people, all of them? And those who disbelieve do not cease to be struck, for what they have done, by calamity - or it will descend near their home - until there comes the promise of Allah. Indeed, Allah does not fail in [His] promise. [13: 31][1].

Allah informed us that guidance is in His hands, giving it to whom He sees deserving. This point alone should be sufficient enough in preventing us from forcing Islam upon anyone. The duty of a Muslim is just to inform.

Thus, the core concept that Allah orders Muslims to practice is never to force Islam upon anyone, since compulsion is a hateful attitude in treating other people. The way that prophets used to treat people from the very start was invitation, and it is the same course which we should follow.

In the Quran, it is stated about Noah (peace be upon him) '*He said, "O my people have you considered: if I should be upon clear evidence from my Lord while He has given me mercy from Himself but it has been made unapparent to you, should we force it upon you while you are averse to it?'* [11: 28][1]. Forcing a belief system upon someone is ultimately irrational since it is unfruitful.

5.8 What reason is there not to depend on Allah?

In the previous section it was discussed how our duty as Muslims is to inform non-Muslims about Allah and Islam, but never to force Islam upon anyone. However, even such basic practice provokes some people to an extent that they are hostile towards those who preach about Islam. Yet this hostility, which could reach the point of assault, should not prevent Muslims from informing people about Islam.

This is because whatever harm that may reach us cannot reach us unless Allah allows it. So we should trust Allah in protecting us, especially since what placed us in harm's way is that we are inviting people to know Allah in the first place. Why shouldn't we trust Allah since we know that he led us to the path of truth and salvation, i.e. Islam, from the start.

And this was the reasoning and attitude of the messengers when threatened while delivering the message of Islam. They used to say '*And why should we not rely upon Allah while He has guided us to our [good] ways. And we will surely be patient against whatever harm you should cause us. And upon Allah let those who would rely [indeed] rely."* [14: 12][1]. If the messengers would have succumbed to the fear of being harmed from others for preaching, Allah's religions would not have been delivered to people (Judaism, then Christianity, then Islam).

5.9 How is it appropriate for a Muslim to be deceitful when he believes that Allah is The-Truth and Islam is the righteous religion?

Since we as Muslims are certain that the path of Allah is the rightful path to follow, then a Muslim should be a model of righteousness in his actions, in order to have credibility. This not only entitles being free from negative characteristics such as being a liar, but entitles a higher level, which is by making our actions conform with what we say.

Any discrepancy between what we say and what we do is a hypocrisy, since a person who claims to follow the The-Truth shouldn't be untruthful, which would be manifested in not abiding by what he says. A man's word is an oath upon him, and a man who betrays his word cannot be trusted. How is it appropriate for a Muslim who believes that Allah is the truth to be deceitful with people through conflicting actions?

And this behavior is no small matter to Allah. *'O you who have believed, why do you say what you do not do? [2] Great is hatred in the sight of Allah that you say what you do not do.'* [61: 2–3][1]. Moreover, how can this person rightfully preach that Islam is the truthful religion, and expect people to trust him, if he himself isn't truthful with his word?

5.10 A Muslim should be generous.

Generally speaking, a Muslim should be generous when spending in the paths which Allah directed us towards. Aspects such as charity, aiding those in debts and in pushing for justice to prevail are greatly rewarded by Allah, considering what great benefit this does in the society. As for those who barely spend in such causes, a very rational concept which Allah confronts us with is this:

And why do you not spend in the cause of Allah while to Allah belongs the heritage of the heavens and the earth? Not equal among you are those who spent before the conquest [of Makkah] and fought [and those who did so after it]. Those are greater in degree than they who spent afterwards and fought. But to all Allah has promised the best [reward]. And Allah, with what you do, is Acquainted. [10] Who is it that would loan Allah a goodly loan so He will multiply it for him and he will have a noble reward? [57: 10–11][1].

This concept is very logical, that when a Muslims balances all the factors, he will find that spending in the cause of Allah is the best investment decision he can possibly make. These factors are: that he will perish and leave behind all his savings one day; that Allah will inherit the Earth and Heavens and all that is upon or within them; that what he spends in the cause of Allah will be multiplied in reward; that what he will spend belongs to Allah in the first place and was bestowed to him as a blessing.

Thus whenever a person is miserly in matters related to what Allah encourages, he is in reality being a miser upon himself. Not only this, but the verse moreover indicates that those who anticipate what pleases Allah and hurry in doing it will get greater rewards. If a person assesses this reasonably, he will notice that this is a perfect system in terms of benefit, fairness, and encouragement.

5.11 Torturing an animal is gravely prohibited, and wasting the resources of sacrificed animals is denounced.

In certain cases, animals are sacrificed as part of a ritual. However, these sacrifices have strict rules to avoid abuse or going astray. Firstly, the sacrifice must be purely in the name of Allah, and not in the name of anything else nor someone with Allah even. There are other rules, such as the prohibition of spreading the slaughtered animal's blood over an object or sacred place, for this does not result in any more protection for the object nor makes it more sacred.

Another rule is that the sacrifice should be of an animal that will be eaten and made use of, such as a sheep or chicken, but never of an animal that will be deserted or discarded. This automatically prohibits the practice of sacrificing animals that are inedible, such as sparrows and cats, especially more for target practice. Animals that are slaughtered for food should be mercifully slaughtered.

These rules are placed to avoid the waste or torture of a living soul. Most of these rules are implied under one logical concept, which Allah stated to us. This concept is: '*Their meat will not reach Allah, nor will their blood, but what reaches Him is piety from you. Thus have We subjected them to you that you may glorify Allah for that [to] which He has guided you; and give good tidings to the doers of good.*' [22: 37][1].

Thus the benefit of a sacrifice is entirely to us, from their meats which we eat, and by the reward from our intention of submitting this sacrifice to Allah (that we will perform this sacrifice under Allah's laws and to strengthen ourselves in worshipping him). Allah will not benefit anything from these sacrifices, but He permits or sometimes orders them for the greater benefit of humans, such as that the meat reaches the poor.

5.12 Non-believers should not be prioritized as trustees.

To a believer, the critical matter of belief in one God is of the utmost importance in life, since he believes that it is the reason he and this Universe were created in the first place. Since the disbeliever has a major error in wisdom, evident while evaluating the most important and obvious issue relating to our existence: God, then how can his judgement be reliable in smaller issues related to life? Therefore, any disbeliever should not be blindly relied upon regarding advice.

And this principle is what Allah wishes to test believers upon from time to time, whether they prioritize the friendship and opinions of disbelievers' over other believers' or not. Allah says *'Do you think that you will be left [as you are] while Allah has not yet made evident those among you who strive [for His cause] and do not take other than Allah, His Messenger and the believers as intimates? And Allah is Acquainted with what you do'* [9: 16][1].

It must be pointed out though that not taking them as trustees is a different issue than not taking them as friends or acquaintances. It also does not mean to take disbelievers as enemies. Disbelievers should not be considered as enemies unless they commit an act of hostility towards believers; only caution is required when interacting with them. It should also be pointed out that this principle does not undermine the knowledge that they have and regard it as wrong, it just means that whatever knowledge they have should be revised before adapting it from them. Many disbelievers have very advanced knowledge especially in scientific fields, which is generally beneficial to humanity.

5.13 Peace with other factions is favoured, but caution should still be upheld.

Islam is a religion that encourages both peace while having strength. Peace alone is not appropriate, as it leads to passiveness and submission when assaulted by unjust aggressors (pacifism). Nor is strength alone appropriate, since we may gradually turn into the unjust aggressors ourselves by becoming greedy, prideful and arrogant.

Some may wonder: if we can achieve peace with other factions, then why is there need to strengthen ourselves? This is because some factions don't respect anything other than strength, which serves as a restraining factor to them, since they comprehend that they will suffer losses if they choose to assault.

It is idealistic to assume that all factions seek peace, or even that all factions will abide by the peace treaties that they sign. Allah directs us to an important fact, that many factions broke their vows with Him of upholding the laws in the scriptures He sent, such as worshiping Him alone if He saves them or sends them a sign. Thus, how can we expect such factions to uphold their vows with Allah's creatures when they violated their vows with Allah Himself?

How can there be for the polytheists a treaty in the sight of Allah and with His Messenger, except for those with whom you made a treaty at al-Masjid al-Haram? So as long as they are upright toward you, be upright toward them. Indeed, Allah loves the righteous [who fear Him]. [7] How [can there be a treaty] while, if they gain dominance over you, they do not observe concerning you any pact of kinship or covenant of protection? They satisfy you with their mouths, but their hearts refuse [compliance], and most of them are defiantly disobedient. [9: 7–8][1].

This is the sad reality, that those who break their vows with Allah are very likely to break their vows with fellow humans, especially when they have the upper hand in strength. And we are given a characteristic identifying feature of them, that when they are the less powerful group, they say reassuring things with their mouths, while their hearts conceal otherwise, seeking an opening to assault or aid those who assault the believers.

Reflecting this upon world reality, what percent of politicians don't lie? Many of them speak of noble causes such as peace, human rights and providing prosperity, while their actions speak contrary to this, such as by selling weapons to criminal regimes or even supporting them with soldiers and funds.

5.14 A Muslim should acknowledge all of Allah's laws.

Some believers may get the impression that it is not necessary for all of Allah's laws to be accepted, which is a very grave mistake. Allah's laws are not a list which we may pick what we like from, it is a curriculum set for us to follow; a guide on how to operate ourselves from the One who has ultimate knowledge and wisdom. Thus, there cannot be an alternate ruling that is superior than His, not even in a single law. This is true faith and submission to Allah: to ascertain that Allah's ruling in a matter is better than personal ruling, and thus prioritizing it in practical life.

Allah sent His guidance in the form of a religion, and when the followers of each religion would neglect their religion and become corrupt, He would send the successive religion to return people to the righteous path. Prior to the arrival of every religion, mankind would had reached a very dire state. The worshipping of idols or even animals was present, eating dead animals was considered natural, adultery was common, women were treated as possessions, men would cut-off their bonds with their parents, neighbours used to harm each other, and the strong used to exploit the weak.

Bottom line, it was similar to the law of the jungle, where the strong is the one who enforces the rules which he desires and benefit him. Thus when a Muslim rejects a certain rule that is decreed in Islam and substitutes it with a human rule, he has in fact brought back a part of the lifestyle of the jungle.

For example, regarding the rule that interest on loans is prohibited. If a person claims that he sees no harm in taking interest on loans, and on the contrary claims it brings a lot of cash to banks which strengthens the economy, he has allowed the strong to eat the weak in a certain field. It is not always about the money, there are humane aspects in almost every matter, which only the wisest can balance.

Another person may not see that adultery should be forbidden, whilst another sees that weapons should not be restricted, and yet another sees that he should not support his parents on the excuse that they should depend upon themselves; each one bringing back a part of the jungle life. In the end we will be living under the law of the jungle again, turning back time to the days when the human race was ignorant and primitive in behaviour, the difference being having advanced technology.

And this is the point which Allah confronts those who want to substitute His laws of guidance: *'Then is it the judgement of [the time of] ignorance they desire? But who is better than Allah in judgement for a people who are certain [in faith].'* [5: 50][1].

It must be pointed out though that there is a difference between rejecting a law altogether and between violating it. Violating a law (whist acknowledging that the law is rightful) is of human nature, since we are flawed beings, and the error will be forgiven by Allah if the person honestly repents. Rejecting a law, however, means that the individual does not believe that this is the wisest ruling, which is a depreciation of Allah's perfection, and this is a fatal flaw in faith.

In this situation, the individual freely violates the rule multiple times on account that he does not believe that it is righteous. In practicality, he has placed his knowledge and wisdom in equivalence with Allah's knowledge and wisdom.

This attitude manifests itself, in terms of actions, in that the individual performs some of Allah's laws but refuses to carry out others. He performs the laws that are easy or go along with his personal desires and benefit, while opposing those that give other people their rights on his account. Allah has mentioned such individuals, indicating that they have a grave flaw within themselves, which a true Muslim should avoid having:

And they say, "We believe in Allah and in the Messenger, and we obey." Thereafter a group of them turn away even after that, and in no way are those ever the believers. [47] And when they are called to Allah and His Messenger that he (The Messenger) may judge between them, only then are a group of them veering away (from it). [48] And in case they truly (have a case), (Literally: they are in the right) they will come up to it compliant. [49] Then is there sickness in their hearts, or do they suspect (Our judgment), or do they fear that Allah may encroach upon them, and

His Messenger (may encroach)? No indeed, those are they who are the unjust. [50] Surely the saying of believers when they are called to Allah and His Messenger that he (The Messenger) may judge between them is only that they say, "We hear and we obey." And those are they (who are) the prosperers. [24: 47–51][2].

5.15 Forbidding something that Allah has permitted is denounced.

Just as a Muslim should refrain himself from doing what Allah forbids, a Muslim should also refrain from forbidding upon himself, or others, that which Allah made lawful. This is because a Muslim is a submitter to the wisdom and ruling of Allah, even if a person dislikes something which Allah allowed. The Muslim may avoid doing what he dislikes from that which is permitted, but has no right to forbid it.

True submission to Allah means accepting and abiding by the laws He set, even if an issue is against the individual's desires. Therefore, when a Muslim modifies these laws, even if by forbidding what is permissible, he is in fact changing his submission that Allah has the sole right of setting what is lawful and what is forbidden. This Muslim has in reality prioritized his judgement and desire over Allah's judgement and will.

Thus, when Prophet Muhammad (may Allah bless him and grant him peace) was about to fall into this error by forbidding honey upon himself to content some of his wives, Allah warned and deterred him from it. Allah said '*O Prophet, why do you prohibit [yourself from] what Allah has made lawful for you, seeking the approval of your wives? And Allah is Forgiving and Merciful.*' [66: 1][1]. This incident set a principle for us.

5.16 Since Allah created us, He knows what secret thoughts and beliefs we have.

This point is a very important point to bear in mind, that Allah sees what we do and is aware of what we think. This is a fundamental point in making people do what is rightful (since rewarding is in the hands of Allah) and avoid what is evil (since it is Allah who ultimately punishes), especially when no one is watching them and won't discover what they will do.

If one logically contemplates upon the fact that Allah created us and the environment which we are in, he will reach the conclusion that Allah knows what we are going to do. If a computer programmer knows what a computer will do, and a chemist knows the resulting product from two compounds he prepared, how can we deny that Allah knows what we will do?

Moreover, since Allah is ultimately superior, He knows even what we secretly discuss within ourselves, to the point that it is equivalent to Him whether we declare our darkest and deepest thoughts or conceal them. Allah informs us about this so that we take it into consideration regarding what we think and do. He says '*And keep your opinion secret or proclaim it, lo! He is Knower of all that is in the breasts (of men). [13] Should He not know what He created? And He is the Subtile, the Aware.*' [67: 13–14][4].

5.17 Being a Muslim doesn't mean being above punishment.

As previously discussed, every religious faction believed that they are the special ones and unique to God, which is a treacherous line of thought. This is because they wrongfully interpreted and applied it, leading them to sinning on account of that they will be bestowed leniency during judgement or even completely forgiven. Muslims should beware falling to this trap, since it is the wishful thinking of every faction to get the greatest rewards for the lowest efforts.

The truth however is that whomever does injustice or corruption on Earth, and harms livings creatures, deserves to be punished irrespective of the nature of their faith. There is no favouritism when it comes to the issue of misconduct, and this is what Allah informs us of *'It will not be in accordance with your desires (Muslims), nor those of the people of the Scripture (Jews and Christians), whosoever works evil, will have the recompense thereof, and he will not find any protector or helper besides Allah'* [4: 123][2].

It is illogical to assume that just because a person is upon the rightful faith in Allah, he has a licence to steal, harm, or kill Allah's creatures, and to disobey Allah generally. How would Allah's justice then be ultimate and effective if He were to overlook injustices that befell on creatures whom He created? And how could a person then be special to Allah when he is doing what Allah hates: corrupting what He created?

5.18 Who wishes to earn Allah's forgiveness?

Due to Allah's grace, there are multiple ways and reasons that may bring about Allah's forgiveness upon a person. One of these ways is incorporated under a general rule: treat people the way you would like Allah to treat you, and love for people what you love for yourself. So if a Muslim wants Allah to be merciful with him, he should be merciful with people. Similarly, if a Muslim wants Allah to be forgiving with him, he should generally be forgiving to the furthest extent with people, even to those who wronged him. Allah stated:

And let not those of virtue among you and wealth swear not to give [aid] to their relatives and the needy and the emigrants for the cause of Allah, and let them pardon and overlook. Would you not like that Allah should forgive you? And Allah is Forgiving and Merciful. [24: 22][1].

In this verse, it addressed a case in which an individual who had wealth swore to cut off the regular aid he used to give to a poor man, after the poor man had harmed him greatly. But since this was an isolated incident from the poor man, Allah advised the wealthy man to resume the aid, especially that the poor man was also a relative of his, on account that Allah is forgiving. This is a very sensible point, that just as an individual is forgiving with Allah's creatures who caused him harm, why wouldn't their creator forgive that individual for the violations he committed with Him?

5.19 An embarrassing inquisition to us from Allah:

Before mentioning my next point, I want to point out how inconsequential we are to Allah. He does not need us, He just advises us to worship Him '*And I did not create the jinn and mankind except to worship Me. [56] I do not want from them any provision, nor do I want them to feed Me. [57] Indeed, it is Allah who is the [continual] Provider, the firm possessor of strength*' [51: 56–58][1]. However, if not a single person worshipped Him He would lose nothing, and yet on the other hand, if every single one of us worshipped Him He would gain nothing.

Moreover, if He gave all the people everything that they ask for, it would only scratch the surface of what He owns, and that is the reality of the situation. This information is delivered to us in a saying (Hadeeth) of the Prophet Muhammad (may Allah bless him and grant him peace), quoting what Allah said to him:

O My slaves, you commit sins night and day and I forgive all sins, so seek My forgiveness and I shall forgive you. O My slaves, you can neither do Me any harm nor can you do Me any good. O My slaves, were the first of you and the last of you, the human of you and jinn of you to be as pious as the most pious heart of any man of you, that would not increase My domain a thing. O My slaves, were the first of you, and the last of you, the human of you and the jinn of you to be as wicked as the most wicked heart of any man of you, that would not decrease My domain in a thing. O My slaves, were the first of you and the last of you, the human of you and the jinn of you

to stand in one place and make a request of Me, and were I to give everyone what he requested, that would not decrease what I have, any more than a needle decrease the sea if put into it. O My slaves, it is but your deeds that I reckon for you and then recompense you for, so let him who finds good (i.e., in the Hereafter) praise Allah, and let him who finds other than that blame no one but himself.[15]

As we see from the Hadeeth, Allah is in no need for us, but we all realize that since Allah created us and provides for us, we are obligated to thank and worship Him. Then why is there a verse in the Quran in which He invites us to worship Him, instead of ordering us, in spite of the fact that He does not need us!? The only logical deduction is that it is for our benefit and not His. The verse is:

Is it not due time for the hearts of (the ones) who have believed to submit to the Remembrance of Allah and that which came down of the Truth, and that they should not be as the ones to whom the Book was brought earlier? Then (their) span became long to them, so their hearts hardened; and many of them are immoral. [57: 16][3].

This is our God, merciful and gracious. He advises us from being like a faction of those who received previous Scriptures and abandoned it, whose hearts became harsher with the passage of time till they turned away from Allah. It is as if He is asking us: haven't we had enough fun and stayed long enough away from Him, so isn't it time to turn to Him? Why does He request that from us when He can compel us to do it? And what will our choice be?

This should be the last chapter in this book since it is based on tangible logic, and together with the previous chapters, they should have guided the reader to the right path. The next chapter, however, requires what I loosely term 'theoretical' logic. To clarify, the previous chapters initiated thoughts and counter-thoughts in the reader, whereas the next chapter is merely an illustration of future incidents projected unto the reader, to strike his core of conscience.

The next chapter, in contrast to all the previous chapters that were aimed at guiding a person, indicates what a person will face if he fails to accept and comply with righteousness. Contrary to what many people would expect, the next chapter will not talk particularly about the reward (Heaven) to those who comply or about the punishment (Hell) to those who defy God. It will simply narrate some incidents that occur between individuals in the Hereafter, incidents that are very realistic from the perspective of logical expectation.

Chapter 6: Conversations that will occur in the future

Although this section contains verses that don't contain a logical statement, I saw that I should mention them in this book because these conversations are very detailed and realistic. They seem logical even from our current experience in life. To clarify, on judgment day when all the people get resurrected, people start to panic over this new unpredictable situation and become horrified from being punished. But God foretells us what people say and how they behave in order to avert ending up in Hell.

And God knows these conversations because He is All-Knowing and unconfined by time, as it is Him who created time for us to be regulated, and therefore He is not bound by the rules of time. The past and the future are one to Him.

Consequently, evildoers will start blaming, lying, clashing and betraying their acquaintances, friends and even lovers, in a desperate attempt of eluding punishment for their sins. But in the end, when all this fails and they realize that they will still be punished, many of them blurt out the raw truth in a final desperate attempt of gaining God's pity for them, and hence His forgiveness too.

And these are all tactics which we have observed individuals resort to when there are prizes to be gained or a penalty that has to befall on someone in this life. We have witnessed such desperate manoeuvres that even reach the point of backstabbing and cheating during competitions over a monetary prize or a job. Similarly, we witness such manoeuvres from some individuals to deter the blame for an error at work, trying to pin the fault on another individual. So imagine when the stakes are even higher, when the prize is Heaven and the punishment is Hell, what lengths will people go to for self-preservation?

On that day, the righteous people who followed the true path and generally did good deeds will be honest with God even about their sins. They wouldn't dare try to lie to God because they know they cannot hide any truths from God, and also from fear of the consequences of lying to God.

In summation, God foretells us of these incidents and situations as an advice so that we take preventative measures in our current life. They are mentioned for us to become precautious from finding ourselves in any of these critical situations, or end up saying what these people said.

6.1 Satan's confession and renunciation

The devil's betrayal reaches its climax on judgment day, for he strived throughout human history to collect the fruits of his labour on this day. Thus when it comes, he disavows himself from all the people that followed him. He does this after he enacted the role of a friend and advisor to people, after he promised them falsely and led them to conceitedness (having too much self-pride from following the truth). He does so because his dream is to lead humankind to eternal Hell, and that is his ulterior motive.

God, advising us, forewarns us of the devil's scheme and his nature, and foretells us of what he will confront us with so that we become wary of his scheme. This is what the devil will disclose on judgment day:

And Satan will say when the matter has been concluded, "Indeed, Allah had promised you the promise of truth. And I promised you, but I betrayed you. But I had no authority over you except that I invited you, and you responded to me. So do not blame me; but blame yourselves. I cannot be called to your aid, nor can you be called to my aid. Indeed, I deny your association of me [with Allah] before. Indeed, for the wrongdoers is a painful punishment." [14: 22][1]. Indeed, what a loss will those that followed him be in.

Then, when the devil's followers realize what he did, they will curse him and despise him. And how not when he led them to doom, but this is a natural consequence for those who turned a blind eye to God's message, which left their souls fertile for the devil to come and flourish upon:

And whoever is blinded from remembrance of the Most Merciful - We appoint for him a devil, and he is to him a companion. [36] And indeed, the devils avert them from the way [of guidance] while they think that they are [rightly] guided [37] Until, when he comes to Us [at Judgment], he says [to his companion], "Oh, I wish there was between me and you the distance between the east and west - how wretched a companion." [38] And never will it benefit you that Day, when you have wronged, that you are [all] sharing in the punishment. [43: 36–39][1].

6.2 All illegitimate ties will be shredded, no matter how strong they were

Prophet Ibrahim (may Allah grant him peace) noticed something very peculiar, that out of social endearment, his townsfolk gathered upon the vain belief of worshipping idols. But whether the reason of this endearment is over-complimenting each other, blind trust in their fathers or pride in their tribe's conviction, all of this will be completely overturned on judgement day. He foretold them this:

And he said: "For you, ye have taken (for worship) idols besides Allah, out of mutual love and regard between yourselves in this life; but on the Day of Judgment ye shall disown each other and curse each other: and your abode will be the Fire, and ye shall have none to help." [29: 25][2].

On that day, the fear is so overwhelming that everyone, including the Prophets except Muhammad (may Allah grant them peace), will be concerned with just their own individual safety from the punishment, for it is a cataclysmic day. These calamitous events cause people to appear drunk from horror, pregnant women to go into labour and children to become grey-haired.

People in general will look for self-preservation to the extent that they do not assist each other; everyone wants to flee with his skin. The evildoers however will be more hostile than that; they will be so desperate to evade the punishment that they will ignore and even sacrifice everyone they know. This comprises their best friends, their wives, their parents and even their children.

And they start to blame themselves harshly for being stubborn and not following the path that the Prophet showed them, and also blame the friends they had that misguided them from the path. God informs us:

And the Day the wrongdoer will bite on his hands [in regret] he will say, "Oh, I wish I had taken with the Messenger a way. [27] Oh, woe to me! I wish I had not taken that one as a friend. [28] He led me away from the remembrance after it had come to me. And ever is Satan, to man, a deserter." [25: 27–29][1].

The final scene, after people have passed through dire events, is that factions will end up in Heaven while others in Hell. Those in Heaven will then greet each other, and some of them will seek friends they can't find after they drifted apart from each other on Earth. Allah informs us:

And they will approach one another, inquiring of each other. [50] A speaker among them will say, "Indeed, I had a companion [on earth] [51] Who would say, 'Are you indeed of those who believe [52] That when we have died and become dust and bones, we will indeed be recompensed?'" [53] He will say, "Would you [care to] look?" [54] And he will look and see him in the midst of the Hellfire. [55] He will say, "By Allah , you almost ruined me. [56] If not for the favor of my Lord, I would have been of those brought in [to Hell]. [37: 50–57][1].

6.3 What each faction says when their book of recorded deeds is handed to them

People should keep in mind that whatever they do is being written down in detail by Angels assigned to each person, and on judgment day, each book is handed to the person it belongs to. This book will be opened and each person will be judged by God on its contents, and the responses ensue. It should be noted that the book is merely tangible evidence on the person; God knows all the details without it.

Those who did good deeds on Earth will be delivered their books in their right hand. The evildoers, however, will try to swindle their way out of receiving their books with their left hand, which happens to doomed people. In a cunning attempt, they place their left hands behind their backs, but it is still delivered to their left hands hidden behind their backs. Hence, every individual initially knows whether he may survive or is doomed according to the hand he received his book with. Here is what every faction will say on a day when all secrets are revealed:

That Day, you will be exhibited [for judgement]; not hidden among you is anything concealed. [18] So as for he who is given his record in his right hand, he will say, "Here, read my record! [19] Indeed, I was certain that I would be meeting my account." [20] So he will be in a pleasant life – [21] In an elevated garden, [22] Its [fruit] to be picked hanging near. [23] [They will be told], "Eat and drink in satisfaction for what you put forth in the days past." [24] But as for he who is given his record in his left hand, he will say, "Oh, I wish I had not been given my record [25] And had not known what is my account. [26] I wish my death had been the decisive one (i.e. his end) [27] My wealth has not availed me. [28] Gone from me is my authority." [69: 18–29][1].

Then their dreadful situation sinks in their minds and they have no choice but to accept the reality they are in, so they open the book to see its contents. They become shocked by how detailed the book is, containing up to the smallest detail that they thought was insignificant. But they also fill with horror since it contains their malicious secrets that they hoped to be overlooked or missed, and contains even the tiniest evil actions which they never imagined they would be judged upon. Everything is mentioned in the book, for a copy was being made of everything they were doing, and God informs us about what they say in fear:

And the Book (of Deeds) will be placed (before you); and thou wilt see the sinful in great terror because of what is (recorded) therein; they will say, "Ah! Woe to us! What a Book is this! It leaves out nothing small or great, but takes account thereof!" They will find all that they did, placed before them: And not one will thy Lord treat with injustice. [18: 49][5]. So alas to those who find their books filled with sins. But they can't blame anyone but themselves, for after all, it is what they did.

6.4 God's judgement of Jesus (may Allah grant him peace).

On judgment day, God will bring Jesus to be judged, and also to clarify to everyone what the truth is from the mouth of Jesus himself (may Allah grant him peace). At that moment, when the faction that claimed that he was God's son (or God himself) hear what Jesus says, their hearts will sink and they will be pinned in horror. This is because it hits them that they will definitely be punished for going along with such stray beliefs. God revealed in the Quran:

And [beware the Day] when Allah will say "O Jesus, Son of Mary, did you say to the people: 'Take me and my mother as deities besides Allah?'" He will say: "Exalted are You! It was not for me to say that to which I have no right. If I had said it, You would have known it. You know what is within myself, and I do not know what is within Yourself. Indeed, it is You who is Knower of the unseen [116] I said not to them except what You commanded me - to worship Allah, my Lord and your Lord. And I was a witness over them as long as I was among them; but when You took me up, You were the Observer over them, and You are, over all things, Witness [117] If You should punish them - indeed they are Your servants; but if You forgive them - indeed it is You who is the Exalted in

Might, the Wise [118] Allah will say "This is the Day when the truthful will benefit from their truthfulness." For them are gardens [in Paradise] beneath which rivers flow, wherein they will abide forever, Allah being pleased with them, and they with Him. That is the great attainment. [5: 116–119][1].

With these verses, God forewarns those who insist on worshipping Jesus (may Allah grant him peace) from finding themselves in this predicament. It is a predicament in which Jesus dissociates himself from those who worshipped him, on the basis that he never asked them to do so. So my advice to who believes Jesus to be other than God's messenger: contemplate about your state, and personally verify the facts from the original untranslated Scriptures.

6.5 The state of the disbelievers

Individuals who claimed that there is no God and no afterlife (atheists) become petrified from the very first moment after their death, because they find themselves in the very state that they denied possible: resurrection. They realize that their life was actually an exam which they neither studied for nor answered, and hence are not prepared for audit during their interrogation in front of God. God informs us about their state *'And [when] the true promise has approached; then suddenly the eyes of those who disbelieved will be staring [in horror, while they say], "O woe to us; we had been unmindful of this; rather, we were wrongdoers." [21: 97]*[1].

What a horrific predicament, for they are certain that their situation is dire and bleak. From the very first moment, they realize that they were wrong and now they have to undergo the judgment phases. And how couldn't they be terrified when God had vowed threateningly previously by saying:

Then woe, that Day, to the deniers, [11] Who are in [empty] discourse amusing themselves. [12] The Day they are thrust toward the fire of Hell with a [violent] thrust, [its angels will say], [13] "This is the Fire which you used to deny. [14] Then is this magic, or do you not see? [15] [Enter to] burn therein; then be patient or impatient - it is all the same for you. You are only being recompensed [for] what you used to do." [52: 11–16][1].

The disbelievers chose the easy and carefree path of enjoying life, and for that they ignored the path of truth and duties toward God. All their deeds were to satisfy their own bodily desires, mainly through sins, and consequently become terrified at the thought of being repaid for their deeds. It is the day which God forewarned about *'Verily, We have warned you of a near torment, the Day when man will see that (the deeds) which his hands have sent forth, and the disbeliever will say: "Woe to me! Would that I were dust!"* [78: 40][2].

In order to fulfil their desires to the fullest, they turned a blind eye to God's signs about His existence, thereby choosing blindness over sight (of the truth). And God is so just that even when He punishes someone, the nature of the punishment matches the nature of the sin committed. So for the disbeliever who chose blindness, God resurrects him blind. This occurs on a day that we are in the direst need of every sense we have, in order to comprehend what is going on around us so that we can try to evade harm. Not being able to assess the situation causes them even more fear. God informs us:

And whoever turns away from My remembrance - indeed, he will have a depressed life, and We will gather him on the Day of Resurrection blind. [124] He will say, "My Lord, why have you raised me blind while I was [once] seeing?" [125] [Allah] will say, "Thus did Our signs come to you, and you forgot them; and thus will you this Day be forgotten." [126] And thus do We recompense he who transgressed and did not believe in the signs of his Lord. And the punishment of the Hereafter is more severe and more enduring. [127] Then, has it not become clear to them how many generations We destroyed before them as they walk among their dwellings? Indeed in that are signs for those of intelligence. [20: 124–128][1].

Then the moment of justice begins, the judgment moment itself, in which they will be audited for their beliefs and actions on Earth. But due to the immense fear, realization that they were obviously wrong, and shame over their beliefs and actions, they are initially speechless from being overpowered and summoned:

And [warn of] the Day when We will gather from every nation a company of those who deny Our signs, and they will be [driven] in rows [83] Until, when they arrive [at the place of Judgement], He will say, "Did you deny My signs while you encompassed them not in knowledge, or what [was it that] you were doing?" [84] And the decree will befall them for the wrong they did, and they will not [be able to] speak. [27: 83–85][1].

But when they will be individually called upon and stand in front of God to be recompensed for their actions, many of them will use the same basic technique of stubbornness that they used with the believers when on Earth. That tactic was to adamantly insist upon their faulty excuses and opinions until others start to doubt themselves or give up.

The problem is, they end up deluding themselves that it may work in various arguments with God also as it worked on humans. God foretells us *'(On) the Day when Allah will make them rise again all together, then they will swear to Him, as they swear to you, and reckon that they are on something. (i.e., they have some standing) Verily, it is surely they who are the liars'* [58: 18][2].

However, their situation is never as dire as when God makes them stand in front of the black, blazing, heavily breathing fire of Hell which they are about to enter, the Fire that they denied existed. God asks them in reproach:

"O company of jinn and mankind, did there not come to you messengers from among you, relating to you My verses and warning you of the meeting of this Day of yours?" They will say, "We bear witness against ourselves"; and the worldly life had deluded them, and they will bear witness against themselves that they were disbelievers. [6: 130][1].

They then sink in regret and in blame of themselves for being so stubborn in life and not believing what they sensed was true. Subsequently, the truth pours out of them in confession at a time when admitting fault is of no avail. God foretells us about their state at that time:

If you could but see when they are made to stand before the Fire and will say, "Oh, would that we could be returned [to life on earth] and not deny the signs of our Lord and be among the believers." [27] But what they concealed before has [now] appeared to them. And even if they were returned, they would return to that which they were forbidden; and indeed, they are liars [28] And they say (on Earth), "There is none but our worldly life, and we will not be resurrected." [29] If you could but see when they will be made to stand before their Lord. He will say, "Is this not the truth?" They will say, "Yes, by our Lord." He will [then] say, "So taste the punishment because you used to disbelieve." [30] Those will have lost who deny the meeting with Allah, until when the Hour [of resurrection] comes upon them unexpectedly, they will say, "Oh, [how great is] our regret over what we neglected concerning it," while they bear their burdens on their backs. Unquestionably, evil is that which they bear. [6: 27–31][1].

They will eventually acknowledge the truth and plea for a second chance in spite of having been warned from judgment day, and after they were advised not to do injustices on Earth. But yet they insisted on taking their own path and impudently challenged the fact that they will be overpowered and judged. This is what God informs us about:

And never think that Allah is unaware of what the wrongdoers do. He only delays them for a Day when eyes will stare [in horror]. [42] Racing ahead, their heads raised up, their glance does not come back to them, and their hearts are void. [43] And, [O Muhammad], warn the people of a Day when the punishment will come to them and those who did wrong will say, "Our Lord, delay us for a short term; we will answer Your call and follow the messengers." [But it will be said], "Had you not sworn, before, that for you there would be no cessation? [44] And you lived among the dwellings of those who wronged themselves, and it had become clear to you how We dealt with them. And We presented for you [many] examples." [45] And they had planned their plan, but with Allah is [recorded] their plan, even if their plan had been [sufficient] to do away with the mountains. [46] So never think that Allah will fail in His promise to His messengers. Indeed, Allah is Exalted in Might and Owner of Retribution. [14: 42–47][1].

God condemns the fact that some of them dwelled in sites of civilizations that God had perished with His wrath, pointing out that their repopulation of an area He doomed previously is considered an excessive audacity in defiance (defiance over defiance). So not only did they disbelieve in God, but they also defied the fact that God's wrath will befall the same place again. They did so although they saw or heard about its incidence before, an extreme defiance and challenging of God.

This together with the fact of their secret plotting to wipe God's word from the face of the Earth, carried out by killing His messengers, distorting His message and hindering people from worshipping Him. The plots were so devious and vile that they, as a metaphor, can move mountains. But Allah sees and foreknows their conspiracies, and He plots for them to overturn their plots, and saves whomever He wills of His messengers from them. Those conspirators were ignorant of this verse:

On the day when Allah will raise them up all together, then inform them of what they did: Allah has recorded it while they have forgotten it; and Allah is a witness of all things. [6] Do you not see that Allah knows whatever is in the heavens and whatever is in the earth? Nowhere is there a secret counsel between three persons but He is the fourth of them, nor (between) five but He is the sixth of them, nor less than that nor more but He is with them wheresoever they are; then He will inform them of what they did on the day of resurrection: surely Allah is Cognizant of all things. [58: 6–7]*[6].

And God consoles us:

Or have they devised [some] affair? But indeed, We are devising [a plan]. [79] Or do they think that We hear not their secrets and their private conversations? Yes, [We do], and Our messengers (i.e. appointed angels for writing a humans actions in the book of deeds) are with them recording. [43: 79–80][1].

So generally, He will aid His messengers towards victory, which is apparent on Earth in that the Holy Books were ultimately revealed and not concealed, and the great Messengers were saved from assassinations. Examples of attempted assassinations that were negated include when Moses migrated through the sea, Jesus was lifted, and Muhammad was informed by Gabriel to emigrate from amongst the conspiring townsfolk (may Allah grant the Prophets peace). And God's victory to His messengers will also be apparent in the Hereafter when everyone that the messengers testify against is thrown in Hell.

But just before they are cast into Hell, they will be humiliated and have their pride shattered further by being made to admit that they deserve punishment for being wrong, after passing through their whole life denying that there is a God and a Hell. God foretells us *'And on the Day when the ones who disbelieved are set before the Fire, (it will be said), "Is not this (really) the Truth?" They will say, "Yes indeed, by our Lord!" He will say, "Then taste the torment for that you used to disbelieve!"* [46: 34][2].

They succumb forcefully on that day to the overwhelming power of God, after they were too arrogant to do so voluntarily in their lives, admitting that Hell is true. They succumb to the point that they testify against themselves that it is justice that they are thrown into Hell for disbelieving in it. Then they will be thrown in Hell, and the Keepers of Hell will reprimand them in the raging Fire:

When they are thrown into it, they hear from it a [dreadful] inhaling while it boils up. [7] It almost bursts with rage. Every time a company is thrown into it, its keepers ask them, "Did there not come to you a warner?" [8] They will say, "Yes, a warner had come to us, but we denied and said,

'Allah has not sent down anything, you are not but in great error.'" [9] And they will say, "If only we had been listening or reasoning, we would not be among the companions of the Blaze." [67: 7–10][1].

And when they are in Hell, they will reflect upon their decisions that led them to Hell and curse the people who led them to this. They will then remorse their defiance of God's signs. We are informed of their state then:

The Day their faces will be turned about in the Fire, they will say, "How we wish we had obeyed Allah and obeyed the Messenger." [66] And they will say, "Our Lord, indeed we obeyed our masters and our dignitaries, and they led us astray from the [right] way. [67] Our Lord, give them double the punishment and curse them with a great curse." [33: 66–68][1]. Moreover, God stirs up their grief at what they missed when they try to repent and ask for another chance at life:

And for those who disbelieve will be the fire of Hell. [Death] is not decreed for them so they may die, nor will its torment be lightened for them. Thus do we recompense every ungrateful one. [36] And they will cry out therein, "Our Lord, remove us; we will do righteousness - other than what we were doing!" But did We not grant you life enough for whoever would remember therein to remember, and the warner had come to you? So taste [the punishment], for there is not for the wrongdoers any helper. [35: 36–37]*[1].

And the people in Heaven wonder about what are the specific deeds that led those people to Hell. They ask them:

In gardens they will ask one another [40] Concerning the guilty: [41] What hath brought you to this burning? [42] They will answer: We were not of those who prayed [43] Nor did we feed the wretched. [44] We used to wade (in vain dispute) with (all) waders, [45] And we used to deny the Day of Judgment, [46] Till the Inevitable came unto us. [47] The mediation of no mediators will avail them then. [74: 40–48][4].

What I want to put particular emphasis on is that they used to wade with the waders, i.e. to be influenced and move along with the crowds in associating with God or disbelieving altogether. Yet that did not keep them safe because the reality is that it wasn't the righteous path, nor was it an excuse for them on judgment day in front of God. Such excuses, that vast amounts of people were doing so also or that it was the other people's fault for misleading them, seem so trivial that day.

So be independent and responsible for your own choices fellow reader, and don't let the wading of people in an unjust issue allure or intimidate you to follow them due to their immense numbers. Every single one of them will be summoned alone in front of God for judgement, so will you and so will I.

As a final word of advice to all disbelievers, the door to rectification is still open from God as long as they are still in this life, for many have been allured by the ample time in their lives and its pleasures. Those people are now in their graves, but unfortunately they did not rectify their state.

This in spite of the fact that God loves repenting individuals, and gives them a special welcome when they return to Him. This is evident in that He orders Prophet Muhammad (may Allah bless him and grant him peace) to deliver a unique message in a unique form. It comes in a form that emphasizes that it is directly from God, symbolizing that a person's repentance is direct between him and God without any intermediaries. That message is:

Say, "O My servants who have transgressed against themselves [by sinning], do not despair of the mercy of Allah. Indeed, Allah forgives all sins. Indeed, it is He who is the Forgiving, the Merciful." [53] And return [in repentance] to your Lord and submit to Him before the punishment comes upon you; then you will not be helped. [54] And follow the best of what was revealed to you from your Lord before the punishment comes upon you suddenly while you do not perceive, [55] Lest a soul should say,

"Oh [how great is] my regret over what I neglected in regard to Allah and that I was among the mockers." [56] Or [lest] it say, "If only Allah had guided me, I would have been among the righteous." [57] Or [lest] it say when it sees the punishment, "If only I had another turn so I could be among the doers of good." [58] But yes, there had come to you My verses, but you denied them and were arrogant, and you were among the disbelievers. [59] And on the Day of Resurrection you will see those who lied about Allah [with] their faces blackened. Is there not in Hell a residence for the arrogant? [39: 53–60][1].

6.6 Those who attributed associates to God

Those who worshipped someone or something which they associated with God will pass through an excruciating experience. It starts during the very first phase of their transferral process to the afterlife, while they are still dying. It starts with how the angel of death greets them during gathering their souls, asking them (in reproach) about the partners they associated with God. God informs us:

Who is more unjust than one who invents a lie against Allah or rejects His Ayat (proofs, evidences, verses, lessons, signs, revelations, etc.)? For such their appointed portion (good things of this worldly life and their period of stay therein) will reach them from the Book (of Decrees) until, when Our Messengers (the angel of death and his assistants) come to them to take their souls, they (the angels) will say: "Where are those whom you used to invoke and worship besides Allah?" they will reply, "They have vanished and deserted us." And they will bear witness against themselves, that they were disbelievers. [7: 37][2].

Subsequently, after they have been resurrected on judgment day, they will be ordered to follow their false deities at a time when these deities themselves are lost. Moreover, the deities relinquish themselves from their followers, since they fear from God in claiming they are partners or equals with Him, thus forsaking the followers to meet their destiny alone and exposed.

God then asks them about how they met His messengers which He sent. '*And (remember) the Day (Allah) will call to them, and say: "What answer gave you to the Messengers?" [65] Then the news of a good answer will be obscured to them on that day, and they will not be able to ask one another.*' [28: 65–66][2].

This while God has ordered His angels to hold them for questioning. He then reproaches them heavily, which makes them start blaming other people:

Then it will be a single (compelling) cry; and behold, they will begin to see! [19] They will say, "Ah! Woe to us! This is the Day of Judgment!" [20] (A voice will say,) "This is the Day of Sorting Out, whose truth ye (once) denied!" [21] "Bring ye up", it shall be said, "The wrong-doers and their wives, and the things they worshipped- [22] "Besides Allah, and lead them to the Way to the (Fierce) Fire! [23] "But stop them, for they must be asked: [24] "'What is the matter with you that ye help not each other?'" [25] Nay, but that day they shall submit (to Judgment); [26] And they will turn to one another, and question one another. [27] They will say: "It was ye who used to come to us from the right hand (of power and authority)!" [28] They will reply: "Nay, ye yourselves had no Faith! [29] "Nor had we any authority over you. Nay, it was ye who were a people in obstinate rebellion! [30] "So now has been proved true, against us, the word of our Lord that we shall indeed (have to) taste (the punishment of our sins). [31] "We led you astray: for truly we were ourselves astray." [32] Truly, that Day, they will (all) share in the Penalty. [33] Verily that is how We shall deal with Sinners. [34] For they, when they were told that there is no god except Allah, would puff themselves up with Pride, [37: 19–35][2].

And if they spot the idols that they used to worship, they will attempt to lighten the burden of their errors by implicating them, to transfer part of the burden onto the idols and in an act of revenge. This is what they will say:

And when those who associated others with Allah see their "partners," they will say," Our Lord, these are our partners [to You] whom we used to invoke besides You." But they will throw at them the statement, "Indeed, you are liars." [86] And they will impart to Allah that Day [their] submission, and lost from them is what they used to invent. [16: 86–87][1].

Another conversation that will take place as God informs us:

And [mention] the Day He will gather them and that which they worship besides Allah and will say, "Did you mislead these, My servants, or did they [themselves] stray from the way?" [17] They will say, "Exalted are You! It was not for us to take besides You any allies. But You provided comforts for them and their fathers until they forgot the message and became a people ruined." [18] So they will deny you, [disbelievers], in what you say, and you cannot avert [punishment] or [find] help. And whoever commits injustice among you - We will make him taste a great punishment. [25: 17–19][6].

That will be the reply of those who were worshipped in general, but they consist of two factions. There is a faction who did ask and encourage people to worship them, contrary to a faction who believed that there is only one God to be worshipped but nonetheless were worshipped by people (as is the case with the angels and with Jesus, may Allah grant him peace). The faction that didn't encourage being worshipped will be exempt from punishment after they reaffirm that they didn't ask to be worshipped:

And [mention] the Day when He will gather them all and then say to the angels, "Did these [people] used to worship you?" [40] They will say, "Exalted are You! You, [O Allah], are our benefactor not them. Rather, they used to worship the jinn; most of them were believers in them." [34: 40–41][1]. Those whom were worshipped unwillingly, such as those who died and were then considered as gods by people, will confront those who worshipped them with a harsh and conclusive truth. The truth

they will speak is that they are so inferior from being a god to the point
that they didn't even realize they were being worshipped:

*And the Day whereon We shall gather them all together, then We
shall say to those who did set partners in worship with Us: "Stop at your
place! You and your partners (whom you had worshipped in the worldly
life)." then We shall separate them, and their (Allah's so-called) partners
shall say: "It was not us that you used to worship." [28] "So sufficient is
Allah for a witness between us and you, that We indeed knew nothing of
your worship of us." [10: 28–29]*[2].

However, the faction that encouraged people to worship them will
eventually have no choice but to admit the fact that they intentionally
led people astray. Yet, when they are sentenced to punishment, they
will still try to pull off the lie that they didn't reach the heinousness of
encouraging people to worship them, and will claim their innocence
from those that worshipped them. God informs us *'Those against whom
the charge will be proved, will say: "Our Lord! These are the ones whom
we led astray: we led them astray, as we were astray ourselves: we free
ourselves (from them) in Thy presence: it was not us they worshipped."*
[28: 63]*[3].

It will then hit the polytheists that their idols betrayed them, and
will admit sorrowfully that their idols relinquished themselves from
their worship. They will do so when asked in reprimand:

*Then it will be said to them, "Where is that which you used to
associate [with Him in worship] [73] Other than Allah?" They will say,
"They have departed from us; rather, we did not used to invoke previously
anything." Thus does Allah put astray the disbelievers. [74] [The angels
will say], "That was because you used to exult upon the earth without
right and you used to behave insolently. [75] Enter the gates of Hell to
abide eternally therein, and wretched is the residence of the arrogant." [40:
73–76]*[1].

In this state, those who associated others with God will employ different techniques, which God knows all of, to avoid being found guilty and hence being assigned punishment. They start with the most basic defensive response, which is denial. God foretells us:

And on the day We gather them together We shall say unto those who ascribed partners (unto Allah): Where are (now) those partners of your make-believe? [22] Then will they have no contention save that they will say: By Allah, our Lord, we never were idolaters [23] See how they lie against themselves, and (how) the thing which they devised hath failed them! [6: 22–24][4].

These lies are in regard to their beliefs. As for their actions, they will also lie that they didn't do wrong deeds, such as causing corruption on Earth or assaulting those who declared that there is just one God. Yet all such attempts are futile in front of God since He knows everything about them, even the secret conversations they had within themselves:

Then on the Day of Resurrection He will disgrace them and say, "Where are My 'partners' for whom you used to oppose [the believers]?" Those who were given knowledge will say, "Indeed disgrace, this Day, and evil are upon the disbelievers" – [27] The ones whom the angels take in death [while] wronging themselves, and [who] then offer submission, [saying], "We were not doing any evil." But, yes! Indeed, Allah is Knowing of what you used to do. [16: 27–28][1].

Then they will all be hurled in Hell, comprising of those who worshiped other than Allah and those who were worshipped but accepted it, asked for it or encouraged it. God reprimands both parties during this phase with a very decisive fact *'Had these [false deities] been [actual] gods, they would not have come to it, but all are eternal therein.'* [21: 99][1]. At that time, the polytheists will confront their false gods with the raw truth, when they are gathered in it and asked:

And it will be said to them, "Where are those you used to worship [92] Other than Allah? Can they help you or help themselves?" [93] So they will be overturned into Hellfire, they and the deviators [94] And the soldiers of Iblees (i.e. Satan), all together. [95] They will say while they dispute therein, [96] "By Allah, we were indeed in manifest error [97] When we equated you with the Lord of the worlds. [98] And no one misguided us except the criminals. [99] So now we have no intercessors [100] And not a devoted friend. [101] Then if we only had a return [to the world] and could be of the believers..." [26: 92–102][4].

And after all of this, they will slyly try to argue their way out of Hell by admitting they were at fault and are repenting, in an attempt to draw God's mercy when the opportunity to repent has long passed. God informs us:

Surely (the ones) who have disbelieved will be called out (to), "Indeed the detesting of Allah is greater than your detesting yourselves, as you were called to belief, yet you disbelieved." [10] They will say, "Our Lord, You have caused us twice to die and You have given us life twice; so we (now) confess our guilty (deeds). Is there then any way for going out?" [11] That is (due to the fact) that when Allah was invoked alone, you disbelieved, and in case (others) are associated with Him, you believe. So judgment belongs to Allah, The Ever-Exalted, The Ever-Great. [40: 10–12][3].

We should notice from the verse the fact that God detests them for associating partners to Him more than how much they detest themselves for not following the rightful path. This indicates that they blame and curse themselves for their stubbornness, stubbornness which reached a level of leading themselves to tremendous suffering. Altogether, an overall view of the process of judgment that polytheists go through is presented to us in these verses:

And indeed We have created man, and We know what his own self whispers to him. And We are nearer to him than his jugular vein (by Our Knowledge) [16] (Remember!) that the two receivers (recording angels) receive (each human being after he or she has attained the age of puberty), one sitting on the right and one on the left (to note his or her actions). [17] Not a word does he (or she) utter, but there is a watcher by him ready (to record it). [18] And the stupor of death will come in truth: "This is what you have been avoiding!" [19] And the Trumpet will be blown, that will be the Day whereof warning (had been given) (i.e. the Day of Resurrection). [20] And every person will come forth along with an (angel) to drive (him), and an (angel) to bear witness. [21] (It will be said to the sinners): "Indeed you were heedless of this, now We have removed your covering, and sharp is your sight this Day!" [22] And his companion (angel) will say: "Here is (this Record) ready with me!" [23] (And it will be said): "Both of you throw (Order from Allah to the two angels) into Hell, every stubborn disbeliever (in the Oneness of Allah, in His Messengers, etc.). [24] Hinderer of good, transgressor, doubter, [25] Who set up another ilah (god) with Allah, then (both of you) cast him in the severe torment." [26] His companion (Satan devil) will say: "Our Lord! I did not push him to transgress, (in disbelief, oppression, and evil deeds) but he was himself in error far astray." [27] Allah will say: "Dispute not in front of Me, I had already, in advance, sent you the threat. [28] The Sentence that comes from Me cannot be changed, and I am not unjust (to the least) to the slaves." [29] On the Day when We will say to Hell: "Are you filled?" It will say: "Are there any more (to come)?" [50: 16–30][2].

In the end, there is a conversation that will occur in the Hereafter which summarizes the sorrowful situation of those who associated partners with God. This conversation was revealed to Prophet Muhammad (may Allah bless him and grant him), who in turn conveyed it to us saying:

Allah will say to the person who will have the least punishment in the Fire on the Day of Resurrection, 'If you had things equal to whatever is on the earth, would you ransom yourself (from the punishment) with it?' He will reply: Yes. Allah will say, 'I asked you a much easier thing than this while you were in the backbone of Adam, that is not to worship others besides Me, but you refused except to associate others with Me.[16]

6.7 How the pure truth is extracted from those who lie

It is unquestionable that various schemes will be attempted by the wrongdoers in order to elude being found guilty, guilty of sins they did commit and are recorded in their book of deeds. They do so because it is futile to give excuses, so the best evasive manoeuver (in their view) is to audaciously deny they did it and shamelessly state that they do not accept their book of deeds as valid evidence over them. Thus they desperately employ the same deceitful strategy with God that they applied with people, which is arguing by falsehood with them.

Now here is the dilemma: how can the truth be extracted from them without resorting to the book of deeds? Surely they won't confess upon themselves, for they have been too vile and the stakes are too high as to come clean now. However, no obstacle can stand in front of God, for He is All-Able over everything, but how God extracts the truth is a truly horrific sight and devastating experience.

Suffice to say that since God is able to do anything and nothing can impede Him, the scenario starts by Him accepting the liar's request, and the book of deeds is dismissed as evidence! Tell me fellow reader, what do you imagine happens next? I will let the Quranic verses speak for themselves:

And on the day that the enemies of Allah shall be brought together to the fire, then they shall be formed into groups. [19] Until when they come to it, their ears and their eyes and their skins shall bear witness against them as to what they did. [20] And they shall say to their skins: Why have you borne witness against us? They shall say: Allah Who makes everything speak has made us speak, and He created you at first, and to Him you shall be brought back. [21] And you did not veil yourselves lest your ears and your eyes and your skins should bear witness against you, but you thought that Allah did not know most of what you did. [22] And that was your (evil) thought which you entertained about your Lord that has tumbled you down into perdition, so are you become of the lost ones. [23] Then if they will endure, still the fire is their abode, and if they ask for goodwill, then are they not of those who shall be granted goodwill. [41: 19–24][6].

Their eyes, ears, skins, hands, feet, all turn against the deniers themselves. These organs not only testify against the soul that ordered them to commit these sins, they also censure the soul, for a discord has occurred between the body and soul!

The Prophet Muhammad (may Allah bless him and grant him peace) further elaborated on this situation, explaining in detail how and why this happens. We are left with no option but to be stunned from these events, up to the point of amazement about how the liar is eventually outmanoeuvred, and wonderment at the criminal's desperate trickery and relentlessness in pointless argument. The narrator of the Hadeeth (conversation) reports to us saying:

We were in the company of Allah's Messenger (pbuh) when he smiled and said: Do you know why I laughed? We said: Allah and His Messenger know best. Thereupon he said: It was because (there came to my mind the) talk which the servant would have with his Lord (on the Day of Judgment), he would say: My Lord, have you not guaranteed me protection against injustice? He (God) would say: Yes; then the servant would say: I do not deem valid any witness against me but my own self, and He would say: Well, enough would be the witness of yourself against you and that of the two angels who had been appointed to record your deeds. Then the seal would be set upon his mouth, and it would be said to his hands and feet to speak, and they would speak of his deeds. Then the mouth would be made free to talk, he would say (to the hands and feet): Be away, let there be curse of Allah upon you, it was for your safety that I contended![17]

When we learn of such events, a spontaneous question raises itself in a person's mind: How dire is a day in which such horrific events

occur? And what more of such horrific events occur which we don't
know about!?

6.8 Arguments between the misleaders and their followers

Some people have a strong personality or strong influences, due
to being rich, famous or occupying a position of authority. Thus, they
are capable of reflecting their opinions upon weaker personalities or
influential people that are fascinated by those who are privileged in
life, and convince them to follow their lead. Usually this behaviour is
practiced for personal benefit of the claimer and therefore detrimental,
such as encouraging the purchase of a certain commodity, the use of
drugs, having extramarital intercourse, or gathering money by any
means without feeling restrained by morality.

This in turns leads to an economic revenue or increased fame for
the claimer, which further adds to his influence and ego. How many
times have governments lied to their general public in order to mislead
them into waging an unjust war in which thousands of people die on
both sides?

And although the followers were misled by these leaders, they still
bear part of the fault of following these detrimental leaders. This is
because they sensed that what the leaders are doing is wrongful, but
were either ignorant or cowardly in opposing them, ending up actually
assisting them in their crimes. And so, in the Hereafter, the followers
try to throw their burden on the leaders, whilst the leaders want to
elude carrying any additional burden over their own. This is what goes
on between them in the Hereafter:

*And they all shall appear before Allah (on the Day of Resurrection)
then the weak will say to those who were arrogant (chiefs): "Verily, we
were following you; can you avail us anything from Allah's Torment?"
They will say: "Had Allah guided us, we would have guided you. It makes
no difference to us (now) whether we rage, or bear (these torments) with*

patience, there is no place of refuge for us." [14: 21][2]. Then, when they witness Hell approximating with their own eyes, their quarrelling escalates:

And [yet], among the people are those who take other than Allah as equals [to Him]. They love them as they [should] love Allah. But those who believe are stronger in love for Allah. And if only they who have wronged would consider [that] when they see the punishment, [they will be certain] that all power belongs to Allah and that Allah is severe in punishment [165] [And they should consider that] when those who have been followed disassociate themselves from those who followed [them], and they [all] see the punishment, and cut off from them are the ties [of relationship] [166] Those who followed will say, "If only we had another turn [at worldly life] so we could disassociate ourselves from them as they have disassociated themselves from us." Thus will Allah show them their deeds as regrets upon them. And they are never to emerge from the Fire. [2: 165–167][1].

The bickering continues, especially between arrogant leaders and their followers whom they led astray by urging them to disbelieve in God or associate with Him partners. This bickering is caused by leaders who conspired to make people stray from the truthful path, and made deviancy appealing to them. The method is similar in concept to the method used by country presidents to trick their citizens into waging war, only to discover after the dust has settled and the damages have taken their toll that they waged a pointless or wrongful war. Such leaders and followers argue on judgment day:

And those who disbelieve say, "We will never believe in this Qur'an nor in that before it." But if you could see when the wrongdoers are made to stand before their Lord, refuting each other's words... Those who were oppressed will say to those who were arrogant, "If not for you, we would have been believers." [31] Those who were arrogant will say to those who were oppressed, "Did we avert you from guidance after it had come to you? Rather, you were criminals." [32] Those who were oppressed will say to those who were arrogant, "Rather, [it was your] conspiracy of night and day when you were ordering us to disbelieve in Allah and attribute to Him equals." But they will [all] confide regret when they see the punishment; and We will put shackles on the necks of those who disbelieved. Will they be recompensed except for what they used to do? [34: 31–33][1].

All that the followers will persistently try to do is to allocate the burden from them to their leaders who misled them, and when they are together thrown into Hell they will try again. They do so in desperation of alleviating the excruciating pain of burning from themselves by any means onto their leaders. But who in his right mind would accept to carry additional pain over his torture? We are foretold:

Behold, they will dispute with each other in the Fire! The weak ones (who followed) will say to those who had been arrogant, "We but followed you: Can ye then take (on yourselves) from us some share of the Fire? [47] Those who had been arrogant will say: "We are all in this (Fire)! Truly, Allah has judged between (his) Servants!" [48] Those in the Fire will say to the Keepers of Hell: "Pray to your Lord to lighten us the Penalty for a day (at least)!" [49] They will say: "Did there not come to you your messengers with Clear Signs?" They will say, "Yes". They will reply, "Then pray (as ye like)! But the prayer of those without Faith is nothing but (futile wandering) in (mazes of) error!" [40: 47–50][2].

When transferring their burdens upon their leaders is rejected, those very leaders who are gravely responsible for their deviation from the rightful path into the crisis they are in, there is nothing left to do in vengeance from those leaders except to insult and damn them. The followers do so by asking God to double their leaders' suffering. God informs us *'And the Unbelievers will say: "Our Lord! Show us those, among Jinns and men, who misled us: We shall crush them beneath our feet, so that they become the vilest (before all)."* [41: 29]*[3].

6.9 How every new 'wave' of people thrown in Hell is greeted by those already in Hell

Every new set of people thrown into Hell curse those in Hell, because they paved the road for them to be disbelievers and encouraged them arrogantly (i.e. the pioneering leaders in blasphemy or sins). At the same time, those that are already in Hell curse the newcomers because they overcrowd Hell. Since Hell keeps getting overcrowded till the evildoers are forcefully jammed in it, this increases their suffering. Hence, the overall situation is reciprocal cursing over cursing. Expectedly, the old residents are repulsed by the entering of the newcomers:

[Its inhabitants will say], "This is a company bursting in with you. No welcome for them. Indeed, they will burn in the Fire." [59] They will say, "Nor you! No welcome for you. You, [our leaders], brought this upon us, and wretched is the settlement." [60] They will say, "Our Lord, whoever brought this upon us - increase for him double punishment in the Fire." [38: 59–61][1].

The old residents curse the new ones also for the fact that they were made to carry (by God) the sins of those newcomers that they misled, and so are tortured more because of their followers who just entered Hell. So it ends up that both those factions keep cursing and damning, moreover asking God to increase the torture of the other group. God informs us about this dreary situation:

(Allah) will say: "Enter you in the company of nations who passed away before you, of men and jinns, into the Fire." Every time a new nation enters, it curses its sister nation (that went before), until they will be gathered all together in the Fire. The last of them will say to the first of them: "Our Lord! These misled us, so give them a double torment of the Fire." He will say: "For each one there is double (torment), but you know not" [38] The first of them will say to the last of them: "You were not better than us, so taste the torment for what you used to earn" [7: 38–39][2].

Overall, God reassures us that this is a natural consequence and befitting justice for the wrongdoers: clashing confrontations with each other under the reality of the situation. It comes *'Indeed, that is truth - the quarreling of the people of the Fire'* [38: 64][1].

6.10 Deceptions resorted to by those in Hell to get out of it

When all is said and done, after the pious people enter Heaven and the evildoers reside in Hell, the people in Hell will resort to various cons and pleas in a desperate attempt to snake their way out of Hell. They behave just as they used to behave on Earth in order to get away with what they desire. Yet these people may not comprehend that they are trying to deceive the God of the worlds, or they may realize it but are too desperate not to try the impossible. In any case, they keep trying as long as they are in Hell.

One of the ruses they try to pull, as God tells us, is to ask that just one day of the punishment be relieved from upon them due to its severity, in an attempt to receive God's pity. *'And those in the Fire will say to the keepers of Hell, "Supplicate your Lord to lighten for us a day from the punishment."* [40: 49][1]. But we all know that if a day is eased from upon them, it will be the start of a series of pleas to get another and another, a ruse to keep every day light. And once they realize that God opened the door of pity over them, they will try to abuse that pity by pleading that He evicts them from Hell.

They will also try to invoke the sympathy and pity of those in Heaven upon them, by calling out for some water which God blessed them with, to reduce the heat and thirst they are in. We are foretold:

And the companions of the Fire will call to the companions of Paradise, "Pour upon us some water or from whatever Allah has provided you." They will say, "Indeed, Allah has forbidden them both to the disbelievers." [50] Who took their religion as distraction and amusement and whom the worldly life deluded." So today We will forget them just as they forgot the meeting of this Day of theirs and for having rejected Our verses. [51] And We had certainly brought them a Book which We detailed by knowledge - as guidance and mercy to a people who believe. [52] Do they await except its result? The Day its result comes those who had ignored it before will say, "The messengers of our Lord had come with the truth, so are there [now] any intercessors to intercede for us or could we be sent back to do other than we used to do?" They will have lost themselves, and lost from them is what they used to invent. [7: 50–53][1] ("We will forget" in these verses means neglect, because God never literally forgets).

And such ruses keep arising continuously from the residents of Hell, till they try the last and most desperate one, the one they hate resorting to because it entails the biggest blow to their pride. The biggest ruse of them all that they will try to pull, when all other tricks have failed to get them out, is to confess with utmost frankness that they were truly evil and that they made a crucial error by not believing. They couple that with a disclosure of regret, in that they now want to amend what they did when given a second chance.

They resort to this as a means of repenting and achieving forgiveness, to reach their true aim which is to get out of Hell by any means. God foretells us that when they are reprimanded, this is what they will say:

"Were not My ayat (Verses, signs) recited to you, yet you used to cry them lies?" [105] They will say, "Our Lord, our wretchedness has overcome us, and we were an erring people. [106] Our Lord, bring us (forth) out of it! So, in case we go back (to disbelief) then surely we will be unjust." [107] He will say, "Begone into it spurned, and do not speak to Me. [108] Surely there was a group of My bondmen who said, 'Our Lord, we believe, so forgive us and have mercy on us, and You are The Most Charitable of the merciful.' [109] Yet, you took them to yourselves (as a target) for scoffing, till they made you forget My Remembrance, and you used to laugh at them. [110] Surely today, I have recompensed them for

*that they (endured) patiently; (and) (i.e., because) they are the ones who
are triumphant." [111] He (Allah) will say, "How long have you lingered
in the earth, by number of years?" [112] They will say, "We have lingered
a day, or part (Literally: Some (part) of a day, so ask the numberers."
[113] He will say, "You have decidedly lingered (nothing) except a little,
if (only) you knew. [114] Did you then reckon that We created you only
for sport and that you would not be returned to Us?" [23: 105–115]*[3].

But God knows that these people are so foul inside that if they
were let out and retested, they would return to their former corrupt
ways. This probably reoccurs as time passes by in their retrial on Earth,
when they get fed up from being bound by righteous rules. It very
likely settles that they eventually plan to use the same con with God
again since it worked the first time. God informs us *'Nay, it has become
manifest to them what they had been concealing before. But if they were
returned (to the world), they would certainly revert to that which they
were forbidden. And indeed they are liars'* [6: 28][2].

And for whomever finds this hard to believe, have we not seen how
a thief or an addict who gets caught by the law repents and vows never
to do that again, but when he is acquitted by the law, many of them
return to their old habits? With some thieves this complete cycle keeps
recurring endlessly.

On a larger scale, God informs us that this happens on Earth
between disbelievers and Him. This occurs when He sends down His
punishment in the form of natural tragedies such as hurricanes and
tornadoes, during which they then pray to Him solely and give Him
vows to become righteous. Yet when the 'natural disaster' passes, they
associate partners to Him as He informed us *'Lo! We withdraw the
torment a little. Lo! ye return (to disbelief)'* [44: 15][4].

Progressively, the residents of Hell realize that these ruses don't
work, yet that doesn't prevent them from reattempting them over and
over due to their immense suffering. They eventually realize that the

only way to end their miserable situation is if they cease to exist, i.e. completely perish. And so, they request from the keeper Angel of Hell to ask God to make them perish from existence, which would still be an escape from the punishment they earned.

But then the Angel keeper replies to them condescendingly *'And they will cry: "O Malik (Keeper of Hell)! Let your Lord make an end of us." He will say: "Verily you shall abide forever." [77] Indeed We have brought the truth (Muhammad SAW with the Quran), to you, but most of you have a hatred for the truth'* [43: 77–78][2]. Hence, they are stuck in monotonous cycles of suffering while they are burning in Hell; truly sorrowful is the state they placed themselves into.

6.11 A conversation that happened in the past that all of us were part of.

All the previous conversations mentioned are destined to occur in the future. However, there is one conversation that happened in the past which we were all involved in, but none of us remember, while God informs us about it. First of all, to those who discredit that it took place, I point out to them how the human memory is treacherous ground, for none of us remember the first year of his life when he was an infant. And most people cannot find a single memory of their childhood earlier than at the age of 3 or 4 for example, although we are certain that we passed through those phases.

Furthermore, sometimes a person is definite that he placed a certain object in a certain place, and yet finds it in another place. He then realizes he had changed its place subconsciously and his memory didn't record it. Thus, the human memory is an elusive source of data. And on that basis, we should ponder when God informs us of this previous incident:

And when your Lord brought forth from the children of Adam, from their backs, their descendants, and made them bear witness against their own souls: Am I not your Lord? They said: Yes! we bear witness. Lest you should say on the day of resurrection: Surely we were heedless of this. [172] Or you should say: Only our fathers associated others (with Allah) before, and we were an offspring after them: Wilt Thou then destroy us for what the vain doers did? [173] And thus do We make clear the communications, and that haply they might return (to the truth) [7: 172–174][6].

God informs us, when He created Adam (may Allah grant him peace) He 'wiped' upon his back, drawing from him all the offspring that was yet to come from him and his children. So Adam (may Allah grant him peace) saw all of his offspring, possibly in soul state, but only God knows. After that, Allah made them all witness that He is their God and there is none with Him. All of mankind concurred with this and stated that they are witnesses about it, as they are also witnesses upon each other, and the Angels are witnesses upon them.

So we and the Angels are witnesses over our acknowledgement that Allah is our God and has no associates, after which He returned all the offspring into Adam's back (may Allah grant him peace). The apparent wisdom that God did so is so that our subconscious memory may act as a guide to us when we see the indirect signs of His existence and His singularity. This will assist us in recognizing, by instinct, that those signs are true, ultimately following His guidance and worshiping Him.

An additional purpose of His informing us with this incident is so that we are precautious from associating partners with God. Ultimately, we can avoid ending up giving various excuses on judgement day for our aberration from the righteous path. So He foretold us as an aid for us to safeguard from finding ourselves falling into this trap and resorting to excuses.

Moreover, the occurrence of that incident is a reference point for us on judgment day. On that day, God returns our memory to us in full so that we remember everything that we did, in preparation to be judged upon them, and to ascertain the truth (for the polytheists). The very logical question remains, why did He let us forget this incident when we descended to Earth?

The answer is very sensible, because if we did not forget, all of the people would have believed in Him as the one and only God. This would render this test of us being on Earth pointless, because the aim of our phase of life on Earth is to see who will obey God and who will disbelieve in Him.

As in regards to why is this life on Earth an exam for us, it is beyond our will and choice, for it is God's will to test us. The purpose of the test is that He wanted creatures that worship Him upon choice while they have the temporary ability of disobeying Him.

Overall, we must comprehend that He is God, He creates what He wills and does what He wills, and it is not for us to question His actions, while He will question every one of us. However, suffices for us to know that He is supremely just in His actions. He has forbidden upon Himself doing any injustice however minuscule, in a situation where no one can enforce this law on Him nor check after Him. He is exalted above needing to resort to injustice.

And there are two additionally important points we need to bear in mind when thinking about why the need for our life on Earth. Firstly, God allowed us to live this life so that when He judges us and anyone argues "I could never do such a heinous act if I lived on Earth", there would be definite proof that he would do it. Not that God needs the proof, but rather out of mercy and fairness, so that the individual would not feel he was done injustice by not being given the chance to live on Earth.

God knows what we will end up choosing to do before we even do it. But it must be pointed out that knowing what we will do does not mean that He forced us to a certain fate, because that would be injustice. The injustice would be in that some people would end up in Hell without being able to do anything about it, but God is exalted and higher than doing an injustice. Knowing and controlling are two different issues.

Secondly, this test is important because the majority of people speak virtuously but not all of them act virtuously; there is a discrepancy between what they say and what they do. To clarify, most people say they love God, but what percentage of them actually does what God loves (what He orders) and refrains from what God hates (what He forbids) generally? A lot of people say they are good people, but their actions speak otherwise.

It is hardship that distinguishes the truly loyal from those that speak virtuously but act heinously. The hardships in this life are the filters of the pretenders from the truthful, those who have only intentions from those who follow through by exerting effort and executing. The concept is similar to how mined rocks are exposed to heat in order to extract precious metals from them. The bottom line is, this test on Earth is essential in the segregation process.

As we saw in this chapter, the situation in the Hereafter is dire, and a person's deeds throughout his life will frame the events he will have to pass through, eventually leading him to his fate (Heaven or Hell). This chapter forewarned us about events that are very plausible, even expectable, to a logically and critically thinking mind, guiding us to the conclusion that the Hereafter is factual and will inevitably befall.

<u>Conclusion</u>

From this knowledge a person has attained, and relating it to actual life, one cannot help but see that it conforms to practical life. An individual can now understand the 'whys' and 'hows' about his existence and that which is around him. Everything falls into place, and we realize that the vast universe that God created is for us to contemplate upon. All this exists so that we recognize the signs of His existence, greatness and Oneness, ultimately guiding us to obey Him willingly.

It all makes sense and we then comprehend the big picture, that we were created to worship Him by choice, which necessitates free will, which will lead to some people doing heinous crimes. Some of those crimes will pass uncaught and unpunished on Earth, but rationally there has to be an ultimate judgmental system that catches even those that escaped on Earth (for this free will to be purposeful).

Otherwise, it will be an unbalanced and pointless system in which every person would ask himself "why don't I do what I like and become a horrible person? Why don't I try to steal, lie, cheat and kill to get what I want whilst evading getting caught?". Thus, chaos would ensue.

So there is a Divine law that keeps us under regulation, the law that we will be judged and recompensed with over our beliefs and actions in this life. Thus, the end result would be a balanced rightful situation, in which everyone has retrieved his right from the other people with utmost precision. And let's be truthful with ourselves, if it wasn't for the punishment that the legal organizations enforce on Earth and the scolding of the people around us about what is right and wrong, crime rates would have risen considerably. We personally would have become more corrupt, even if it was in moral matters such as betraying or lying.

Similarly in concept, but on a more Divine level and with a perfectly accurate justice system, God sent us laws for us to abide with. Part of these laws guides us as to how we should worship Him, while the other part guides us as to how we should treat the people around us and preserve ourselves. Failure to comply will lead to a punishment from God, depending upon the nature, severity and frequency of the defiance, which will mainly be in the Hereafter. And the basic rule that we will be judged by is summed up in this verse:

What! Do those who seek after evil ways think that We shall hold them equal with those who believe and do righteous deeds, - that equal will be their life and their death? Ill is the judgment that they make. [21] Allah created the heavens and the earth for just ends, and in order that each soul may find the recompense of what it has earned, and none of them be wronged. [45: 21–22][5]. So this is the ultimate truth, the ultimate reality.

Lastly, a personal word of advice to those who find this book (or parts of it) challenging or intriguing: try to reread it. This is because the book was intended to be brief but intricate. Sections may complete each other, sometimes in other chapters, by elaborating further on aspects of a topic, whilst other sections may require previously mentioned information to be fully comprehended.

Biography

The author was born in 1979, and is currently working as a dentist in Egypt. He discovered that there was more to life than just living, there was maintaining a connection with the Creator: Allah. He wanted to contribute to Islam, and so he wrote this book (which is his first). The aim of this book is to direct people to the path of salvation by using their minds, since the author himself was previously a victim of public trends and propaganda that led him astray.

He loves logical thinking and civilized rational debating, and believes that the mind is a blessing that should be put to use. This is essential since when we will be judged by God, everyone will be judged alone based on his decisions. One of his main principles is: don't deny a truth even if it is against your interest or hurts your pride, no matter how hard admitting it is. And declare the truth as soon as possible, for denying or resisting it causes harm to one's self mainly.

Contact details: hat_em@hotmail.com

References

1 Sahih international

2 Muhsin Khan

3 Dr Ghali

4 Pickthall

5 Yusuf Ali

6 Shakir

7 Musnad Ahmad 17209

8 Sahih Muslim 3431

9 Sunan Abi Dawud 3052

10 Sahih Al-Bukhari 5514

11 Sunan Al-Nisa'i 3104

12 Sahih Muslim 2286

13 Musnad Ahmad 22978

14 Sahih Muslim 2564c

15 Sahih Muslim 2577

16 Sahih Al-Bukhari 6557

17 Sahih Muslim 2969

www.ingramcontent.com/pod-product-compliance
Lightning Source LLC
Chambersburg PA
CBHW071940150726
47999CB00001B/268